ESCAPE FROM STALAG LUFT KERNOW

Written by James Christie

WOW Book Publishing™

Dedication

Many, many thanks to Pauline, my sincere book angel, for finally helping to get my book published

Copyright Page

First Edition Published by James Christie

Copyright © 2021 James Christie

WOW Book Publishing™

ISBN: 9798561730108

All rights reserved. Neither this book, nor any parts within it may be sold or reproduced in any form without permission.

No part of this book may be reproduced in any form or by any electronic or mechanical means including information storage and retrieval systems, without permission in writing from the author. The only exception is by a reviewer, who may quote short excerpts in a review.

The views and opinions expressed in this book are that of the author based on his personal experiences. The author, being cynical and sarky, does not guarantee that anyone following the techniques, suggestions, ideas or strategies will become successful. So good luck with that.

The author shall neither be liable nor responsible for any loss or damage allegedly arising from any information or suggestion in this book. Which is good because the author wouldn't give two figs about people taking the content in the book the wrong way anyway

PART ONE: Prelude-An Ill Wind Blowing in 2007

This is the story of me.

Or rather, a selection of interlinked stories in a difficult period in the life of me. From a person always considered unusual or weird by ordinary ignorant casual trendies. Because of me refusing to abide by society's rules and regulations and today's over the top political correctness. For refusing to conform for what you're supposed to 'wear' or 'look' in life.

For just being *myself*.

JANUARY

At the beginning of the new year, 2007, it was the same old bollocks, really. No girlfriend, no job, bugger all dosh, stuck in a rut. I had been punk for around 15 years, going to various gigs up and down the country and abroad in some cases. For me, punk was always hypercritical whereas it was supposed to be fun: it is, or supposed to be anti-establishment and certainly anti political correct. But yet, half these punks that were acquaintances or loosely termed 'friends' of mine would come out with the most pathetic racist shit or political crap ever. Me not being white anyway, my heritage being Jamaican but never once felt Jamaican as I was born and raised a South Londoner. (A good one for the bigots would be to say Jamaica at one point in its' history was a British colony so therefore part of the British Commonwealth. So when they start to spout crap like *"There ain't no black in the Union Jack"* tell 'em to stick that quote up their arse.)

I was getting pretty disillusioned with the whole punk thing and punk gigs as it was now once again turning into a violent scene reminiscent of when I first got into it at the tail end of the 1980's. In the London scene in particular, which I was part of, it would be considered unusual *not* to see a punch up at a gig. In fact, every time I went to just about any gig there was always some wanker kicking off. And the usual back-biting and slagging.

And for me the most irritating statement imaginable:

"You're the first black punk/skinhead I've seen."

This would almost always lead to the following poxy set of questions always asked by stupid ignorant white foreigners and other people over the age of about 25:

"Where do you come from?"
"South London, originally."
"But where do your PARENTS come from?"

German people would be even more ignorant. But then again, that's just about typical of those sorts of people.

"Bist du aus Afrika?" ("Are you from Africa?")

You would've thought that in this day and age, they'd be no room for such ignorant shit like that, but you'd be surprised. So, bit by bit I gradually got out of the scene. I stopped putting on local gigs. I stopped producing a crappy DIY zine called "Stick Two Fingers" I did on and off for 10 years. Concentrated more on going to ska gigs and Northern Soul nights.

Shaved my barnet off.

Became skinhead.

Felt bloody good about it, too.

All my life I have felt and looked alternative. That is, alternative to other people who consider themselves 'normal', whatever that means in this messed up world of ours. You could say I'm still an Angry Young Teenager still trapped in a 38 year old body with absolutely no intention of growing up responsibly wotsoever. And unless this useless, bigoted, fucked up society changes...and that ain't ever going to happen in my lifetime, no sir- I shall always look, dress and think alternative.

So here I was at the beginning of, according to Christianity and some bullshit concept called God, the year of "his lord almighty, the Jesus fucking Christ" 2007 (you'll also notice that I am an extreme atheist and extremely proud of that fact) in a rut, with no prospects...nothing. One day, while just relaxing at home, home being a tiny, shitty, one bedroom ex-council flat in Beckenham, in the outer suburbs of South London, where if I had any guests, they would have to go through my bedroom to get to the bathroom, such was the way these stupidly designed flats were built, and now taken over by the Glorious Broomleigh Housing Association (a.k.a. Total Money Grabbing Piss Taking Bunch of Wankers), while (I think I was chatting to someone on me computah as usual), I gets this call from an old Czech mate of mine called Daniella who had stopped going to punk gigs a while back.
It went a bit like this.

"Mick, are you still single?"
"Yes."
"I have a friend of mine who I think wants to meet you. Here's her Myspace address. Give her a message."

Ah! Myspace. Before Facebook became massive, there was Myspace. The scourge of all internet romances, where you can make or lose friends in an instant. Where gossip is rife, where the whole world seems to read your messages without you knowing about it. Lost a few friends on there, meself. Don't really give a fuck anymore either.

The person in question, Daniella's mate was a Czech woman called Barbara, in her late 20's. We'd leave messages for each other which gradually led to IM (instant messaging via MSN Messenger) which led to swapping phone numbers which finally led to arranging a date. It was her idea, I think.

She lived and work in an extremely posh green belt area called Chalfont St Giles, a place so disgustingly upper class, it made the posher parts of Beckenham look like the Aylesbury Estate at the Elephant and Castle. Twenty miles out of London and one of the last outposts on the Metropolitan tube line. I met her at the station and then went to a Thai restaurant where we had some of the most delicious and mouth- watering food imaginable. The date seemed to have worked out fairly well as we enjoyed each other's company.

Personally, I thought she looked stunning, even better than her Myspace profile: slightly rounded face with a pale complexion; cute small nose, shoulder length dark hair and slightly large, but full lips which when she smiled, she pouted which made her look even more attractive.

FEBRUARY *The One That Got Away*

Y'know, I was never too good at relationships, me. Before getting to know Babs, as I liked to call her, none of my previous relationships, except my first love, ever lasted more than two months. Maybe it was me. Or maybe it was them who thought of me as "Oh, that Mick seems like a good laugh" but then get tired or bored of me after a short while. Hm.
   I shrug to myself.
Babs, as it turned out to be, was no different, either.

Chrissy is and always will be my best female friend. She was punk for years like I was and was in several bands. After years of wasting my time trying to get her attention affectionately, I gave up, but she's still my best friend, even though we now live hundreds of miles apart across England. She's like a kind of soulmate I never really had and can console each other when we're down and have a great laugh when we're in better spirits.

"So who's this Czech woman you're going out with then?" she enquired. "I'm really happy for you!"

"Oh, her name's Barbara. I feel like I'm the luckiest bloke in the world, but I give it two months, tops."

"Come on now Mick, be a bit more positive..."

"Well you know yerself wot a disaster I am with relationships. Two months, tops," I replied erstwhile.

I'd always had a thing for Chrissy. We'd met several years ago when she was fronting a now defunct punk band called Concussion back in the mid 1990's. She had wild blonde hair then, with killer looks and was fairly well built (not fat as in Anne bloody Widdecombe, just... well built.) Chrissy always used to put herself down about her weight which I could never understand (must be a woman thing) because she really was and still is a stunner and I'd get annoyed with her and tell her to stop slagging herself off. She's a very talented singer in her own right but you know how it is with just about all DIY bands; she and the band never really got anywhere.

Mind you, she was a bit of a snob when it came to choosing men and always the wrong ones too, which led to more unhappiness than happiness, but it was through her that I met Haggeston, from Hamburg. One of three Germans I know that can speak flawless English extremely fast without an accent. Ah, many were the happy times when we'd go on 'hair of the dog' sessions (missions!) after a good piss up, either at his place in Haggeston (hence the nickname, from a Hackney suburb in East London) or at my flat in Beckenham. But enough of this banter, that's for some other time...in another book...

...so things were going fairly well between me and Babs and she arranged to go out for a drink with me about a week later at a pub on the Finchley Road, near Swiss Cottage. She had to catch a flight from Stanstead to the Czech Republic that night so we had some time to kill. We had a good old natter about...well, stuff...and a good drink.

   Next thing I know she turned my head round in her warm hands and we kissed...which turned into an almighty songfest which seemed to last an eternity and it didn't seem to matter to her not one bit that we were doing it near a group a five or six trendies who were drinking and chatting quietly amongst themselves. When I eventually came up for air some moments later, I looked at her blankly for a few seconds, then realised with a grin on my face that this really *was* reality and not fantasy for once.

   Shortly after, we walked to a bus stop where she didn't have to wait too long for her bus to Stanstead. Another mini songfest...hugs...kisses. It was quite a wonderful night to remember, really. It's one of them special moments that'll you'll always cherish forever long after a relationship has ended. I waved her of the bus and off it went, trundling away, into the night.

   We had pre-arranged that I'd meet her at Stanstead a few days later on her return trip back from the Czech Republic. Or was it Slovakia? Well, it's all Czechoslovakia to most people anyway. A few hours before, I was relaxing in a nice warm bath and I had my mobile near the rim (tut tut-silly billy.) Now before this, I'd only had a mobile barely a month as I can't stand the poxy things and I can't stand the poxy people using those poxy things. But even I, shit-for brains, shoulda realise you DON'T put a mobile phone near water.

 Because wot happens?

Ah-HAA! You guessed it, mate.

It dropped into all that lovely, bubbly, soapy water.

   I picked it up in a flash but of course the damage had already been done. Now wot? Wot would happen if there was an emergency and I couldn't contact Babs? Shit, shit,shit,shit,shit,shit,shit......

With this worrying thought lingering in my head, I got dressed quickly and headed off to Stanstead.

Tube up to Tottenham Hale, a few minutes later, on aboard the Stanstead "Express". I do my usual train bunking stint and hide in the smelly bogs. Well look, it's gotta be done, innit? If those sad bastards wanna pay a whopping £15 return ticket just to travel to some airport barely 30 miles outta London, that's their tough bollocks.
Bab's plane was one of the last to arrive at the airport for the night. Typically, it arrived late anyway and she was the last person to arrive through customs. I was getting more and more agitated the more I waited as I saw everyone past customs except her, but when she finally did turn up after a lengthy wait, I wasn't half relieved.
There were no last trains back to London so we got a coach back into London and got off at Victoria. We decided to return back to my flat in Beckenham so we walked to Whitehall and got a N3 night bus which took about an hour.

As the relationship continued, it seemed to be going fairly well for the time being. Once, we were having a good old shagging session at her place (as you do) and it was one of the rare occasions that I came and had a fantastic climax. But then she immediately burst into tears and I asked her what the bloody hell was the matter with her.

"Too young to be having kids" she murmured, or words to that effect. But since she was supposed to be on the pill, I thought that would've been the last thing on her mind (*don't be so bloody naive, Micky*) so the next morning she insisted on lending me her bike and for me to go to every GP practice and chemist in the village, a good mile and a half away, to get some contraceptive pills.
Her bike was half a foot too short for my usage and she didn't have any tools for me to adjust the saddle spoke, so it made cycling extremely difficult and uncomfortable. I rode into the village and I must've looked a right wally when I asked for what she requested-how was I to know by law (apparently) a male partner wasn't allowed to

purchased pills for his missus? I phoned her this news by mobile and then returned to her place, but halfway by tube because there was just no way I could ride the whole distance home on her bike.

   As the weeks dragged on, I found the partnership was becoming more and more strained. Due to her work commitments as a live-in carer she couldn't visit me in Beckenham and I was becoming fed up of always having to visit her in Chalfont which meant having to change trains at Farringdon and always in the evening rush hour too which was just a fucking nightmare.
   However, she'd take me to restaurants and while that was all very nice and jolly, it wasn't really my thing; she was also trying to change me into something I wasn't really comfortable with (fashion-wise, that is) and no way was I going to accept that.
   I took her to a punk gig once up Camden way to see a Yank band called The Casualties. She seemed to have enjoyed that; snogging the arse of each other at the back of the venue while everyone else at the front was going berserk pogoing and stage diving. I think that was the last time I seriously enjoyed her company.
   Things came to ahead when we were supposed to go for a quiet drink at a pub called The Commercial, opposite Herne Hill station one afternoon. She had seemed offish and abrupt when we had talked on the phone a day previously so I was expecting the worse. At the pub she was strangely quiet and withdrawn and while she was drinking she seemed so subdued I couldn't make out half the words she was saying.
   Then the penny dropped.

"I don't think I can go out with a man that drinks so much."

Ever heard of the 'lead balloon effect' where you puncture the balloon, there's a loud 'bang' and it drops to the ground rapidly? Or in some comedy films or tv shows where there's a sound of a record loudly scratched and then dead silence when someone has said something totally out of order? That's how fast my heart sank.

I looked at her quizzically for a moment querying why she had said such a hypercritical question like that, seeing she likes a fair old drink herself.

"I'll cut down. I'll only drink at the weekends."

I'll admit I love being a pisshead. The only difference with me is that I have never become leary or start fights after a few drinks, but it seemed she had already made up her mind long before we had bothered to go to the pub together and long before this pointless conversation had even started. It wasn't long before we got up and left the pub and I uncomfortably walked with her back to the station, where I saw her on the train back up to London and I went in the opposite direction to home somewhat dumbfounded and confused.

I suppose that was the beginning of the end of the relationship, really-well, it certainly was when I left a Myspace message to a friend of mine cryptically quoting "soon to be ex-girlfriend" *(foolish, FOOLISH! Don't you EVER learn, Mick!)* and of course she reads it, as does every other fucker in the world does, regardless of the fact it was sent as a private message and then she has the utter front to accuse *me* of dumping *her*!

Ah. When I fuck things up, I really go the whole hog, me! But what the hell, I thought we could at least discuss how the relationship went wrong on both our parts and what we could do to sort things out but, hell, I wasn't even given the chance to even do that. Wished the selfish bitch had told me that a whole two months ago and saved me the bloody bother of yet again stupidly falling in love because she didn't seem to have wasted much time finding a new bloke either by the looks of things. Fucking typical.

I really did like Babs. But I suppose like always, it just wasn't meant to be. I know now that she was only trying to help me out in her own way but I was too blind to realise this at the time as I thought she was just interfering.

Years later, when I reflect on what could've been, a close friend once said to me: "Mick, think of all this as the following: don't think you've lost a girlfriend, think of it as her losing a decent fella."

And she was right.

* * * * * * * * *

SPRING AND SUMMER: THE ADVENTURES OF KRAUT BITCH
PART ONE: *Internet romance*

There was then a three month period when nothing much was happening in my life again. I'd still go to the odd gig to meet up with friends and get wasted, but even that was on the wane. The usual bollocks. Then one day out of the blue while replying to Myspace messages (ahhh! Wonderful bloody Myspace, it's THE site for really great slagging and bitching, y'know), I received a curious request from someone calling herself "Flaming Star" wanting to add herself to my friends list. I checked out her profile details first and she seemed a pretty decent person to have a chat and laugh with. Within a week we'd not only exchanged messages on a regular basis but were chatting everyday on a 'messenger' called Skype (a bit different from the usual Yahoo and Hotmail MSN's). Within a fortnight we'd be talking on the phone a lot or via a webcam. She requested that she wanted to learn some typical London slang so I started teaching her what I called *"Cockneysprache"* which was a whole shitload of fun.

"Flaming Star" in question, was a young German woman called Danie from the city of Dusseldorf who was a former skingirl with her main musical interest being Doo Wop. Doo Wop is basically rock 'n' roll ballads of the late 1950's and early '60's to which I find the majority of them bloody crap. The name "Flaming Star" itself is the name of an Elvis Presley love song.

For the second time in my life, I found myself truly falling in love with a woman I'd never actually met. We'd chat for hours during the night almost every night solid and the chats became more and more intense and serious. This went on for about a month and a half and then one night I suggested that since our birthdays landed on the same week in July, I could come over to Germany and visit her for some days and have a double celebration.

She seemed overjoyed about this and I was eagerly waiting to meet her at long last. But this wouldn't be for another three or four weeks. I'd write her limericks and love poems which she loved (I used to have a knack of thinking up and writing poems on the spur of the moment) and as the chats went on, becoming even more intense, I'd end up with tears in my eyes as almost all the conversations were very emotional.

But I wasn't prepared for the days ahead when I did finally meet up with her...

When I told her that I had to attend an induction period at a new college called St Loyes in Exeter, Devon that I'd be attending later in the year she revealed she would go berserk if she didn't hear from me. I was there for three days and we kept in touch via Skype messenger. It was during this induction period that I met a person from West Cornwall called Gill. More about her later in this book.

* * * * * *

THE ADVENTURES OF KRAUT BITCH, PART TWO *Mind games and emotional blackmail*

"*Follow your heart*", she said to me once. She also said to me "*don't you ever change the way I am.*" or she'd never speak to me again. If I could've foreseen the trouble and mental heartache which lay ahead before coming to Nazifascistsiegheiling Land, I wouldn't have bothered. I'm no fortune teller but surely the omens were there to see, seeing I'd been to that god awful country on eight separate occasions and I'd get grief and dirty looks from the local whites, the German Turks, who must rate as one of the most ignorant set of complete cunts in the world, as well as German blacks. I'm not too sure just what their problem is, but they can all just go to hell, the lot of 'em.

This occasion wouldn't be any different wotsoever, but seeing as I've visited Germany (spit) so many times you would've thought I'd be able to speak the poxy language fairly fluently. That's if I'd bothered to learn the bastard thing properly.

Which I didn't.

My excuse?

It is extremely difficult for anyone to self-teach himself any language, despite language tapes, cd's and books. Unless you have too much time on your hands and are totally dedicated to be in a set routine which very few people are due to work commitments. Secondly, what you are taught in school doesn't usually reflect what is actually spoken in that country as many people speak in slang and of course with different regional accents and dialects, what you might have learnt might not be understood properly from region to region. And thirdly, it's always best to spend some time in the country of the language you are trying to learn. I can get by on a few sentences, but I must admit, I could be a lot better.

The first three or four days hanging out with Danie was just pure riot. She's a great fan of British film and tv humour (like all my German alternative mates are) so I got her some pressies in the form of several videos, one of the them a recording of 'A Shot In The Dark', the second and best of the Pink Panther series of films. We were absolutely pissing ourselves every time we'd watch the video and use to act out several bits of dialogue or scenes. There was one memorable time when we went shopping together at the nearby hypermarket, an absolute monster of a shopping complex, where we did just that, but changed the words slightly so it went a little like this, I acting as Inspector Clouseau and Danie as his long suffering assistant, Hercule:

   "Facts, Danie, FACTS! We are at a hypermarket. FACT! You are pushing a shopping trolley. FACT! And we are about to do some shopping. FACT! What, then, is the inevitable conclusion I have deducted?"
   "That, er, that we are indeed about to do some shopping?"
   "But of course we are going to do some shopping, you...y-you FOOL!" (much emphasis on the last word).

   Everyone has their favourite moments or times in their lives and even though we are no longer together, this period in my much maligned life was of my all-time faves, ever.

   However, it was on the night of a trip to a local pub in the centre of Dusseldorf that things rapidly started to decline.

   Tonight was a DJ night playing music of a variety of sorts (it was meant to be "alternative" but the rubbish the DJ was mostly churning out couldn't have been more "alternative" if it came up to him and bit him on the arse; the set started well enough at first, including "One Step Beyond" to which me and Danie were the only ones on the dance floor doing some utterly serious skanking. Another all-time favourite moment of my life.

We sat for a bit of a breather; she then accused me at looking at 'other women'.

Wot the hell? Where the bloody hell did that come from?

   Oh great, that's all I need, another insecure nutter for a missus, I thought.
   She went off in a huff to chat to some friends of hers and I decided to mingle elsewhere, anywhere would do so I could avoid listening to the dreadful pap the DJ was churning out. And besides, I'd ran outta beer and I needed a top up, expensive as it was.
   The music really was getting more and more fucking rubbish so I went upstairs and got into conversation with a barmaid and several other people. When she came back upstairs apparently wondering where I was and saw me chatting to the barmaid, she literally exploded.

   "Here's your coat. We're going."
   "What're you talking about? I thought-"

   Suddenly, without a word, she took my arm and stormed out of the pub. It had begun to piss down heavily, so we began the 20 minute walk back to Danie's flat in complete silence.
   Halfway towards home we stopped off at a bus/tram stop to have a fag and I think we must've uttered all of about four words between us before continuing the walk.
   We got home, drenched, the water literally running down us in streams. We glanced at each other now and again blankly, still without a word being uttered. The atmosphere was thick with uneasy tension and in the end I couldn't stand it any longer and went to bed alone for the first time in four days.
   The next day I got up fairly early and had a shower. It was a day before her upcoming birthday and I had wanted to visit a friend in Aachen. Only unfortunately, once again things didn't quite work out the way I wanted it to. I had tried to contact my friend earlier but he

wasn't available. I asked Danie if she wanted to come with me, but she muttered some excuse of getting out of it which was just as well as I travel better alone anyway.

I walked to a local station which was only a few minutes' walk from her flat and patiently waited for a train into town and then a connecting train to Aachen. As I sat down to read a book, who should pop up but one of Danie's friends...whom I've long since forgotten his real name but he was apparently one of the first ever Dusseldorf punx way, way back when it all kicked off in '77. Funnily enough he bears a startling resemblance to Jello Biafra out of fan faves Yank punk outfit The Dead Kennedys. So, for this book's purpose, he'll be called 'Biafra.'

* * * * * * * * * * *

He had spotted me after I had left Danie's flat. He had then followed me to the local railway station. But was he an angry ex keeping tabs on me? On the platform I explained that I was still in a pretty foul mood after what had happened last night. He persuaded me to forget about the trip to Aachen (the chances are was that it almost certainly would've been a wasted trip anyway seeing as he probably wouldn't have been at his flat) so we went back to his small apartment speaking in broken German and half English along the way. It was quite something else, chatting away in two languages.

Now it has to be said that the majority of German apartments and flats, certainly the ones where all my friends live, are pretty basic and small and not much difference in space compared to most English one–bedroom flats. This included Biafra's flat. In the meantime he had prepared a small but mouth wateringly delicious German dish consisting of some meat and this rather curious purple veg, all washed down with some excellent strong lager.

Later on that afternoon I met his parents who were originally from Eastern Europe somewhere. For some ignorant, uneducated reason his mum thought I was an Arab/Muslim and that was beyond being fucking insulting, it was downright bang out of order, but then again, that's the sort of ignorant shit you'd expect from people like that.

Germany. What a wonderful place, eh.

Once they left, and good riddance to bad trash, we carried on drinking.

Now, like all Germans, he's in a league of his own when it comes to boozing. Hardcore just isn't the word.

We downed a few more bottles while bitching about Danie, and then went to see some friends of his near the central area for an hour or so. It was approaching dusk and I knew Danie was beginning to wonder where I was. To tell the truth, in my frustrated state, I wasn't really too bothered about how she felt about me at the moment. Anywhere would do apart from her place for the time being, but then I realise I was just being irrational and selfish to myself and common sense began to creep in gradually, so I trundled back to her place three hours after I said I'd return back.

To best put it mildly, she weren't too pleased when I finally arrived. When I told her that I was with her best punk mate, she got into somewhat of a strop. In fact, she was so enraged that he hadn't rang her to say I was with him, she rang him up and had a full blown argument over the phone with him saying to me later he's done this thing before with other male mates of hers (obviously a jealousy streak thing on his part.) She actually wanted to go over to Biafra's gaff to give him a good smack and I now I blame myself for the breakup of her friendship with him. Not a very nice ending to a day in which I quite enjoyed...without her company.

The next day, it was Danie's birthday and I thought at least for the time being that things between us would be a little better, surely. Hell, I couldn't have been more wrong. We started to bicker with each other almost immediately after day break when I had wanted to visit Haggeston in Frankfurt for a couple of hours and then return back to Danie's as she was going to have a little birthday get-together with her mum and some friends. Now I'm not one for being tactful and sensitive at the best of times, believe me, but her response was somewhat startling to say the least:

"You don't love me anymore."

She had started to play 'mind games' with me and I wasn't going to stand for that.

"Danie", I began, and it seemed with every fourth word I spoke my voice began to rise as my anger began to boil. "If I didn't love you, why would I've travelled 600 miles all the way to Germany to see you and give you presents?" I banged my hand on her wooden table, startling her. This was the one and only time I have ever been that angry with any woman. My eyes started to fill with tears.

"Come here." She beckoned.

We embraced each other and for a few precious seconds shared a pivotal and tender moment. Between this and the period immediately before her birthday bash, it was largely uneventful, but when Danie's mum turned up, we had such a laugh (I now know where Danie gets her humour from) even though with my shit pigeon German and she only speaking a couple or so words of English we somehow understand each other. She specializes in *"Pflaumenkuchen"* (plum cakes) and like all German food, it was absolutely delicious. But as the evening wore on and the more everyone was socializing and boozing, Danie and I mistakenly thought we were both ignoring each other. We kept on exchanging odd glances, when suddenly she got up and stormed off, went inside her flat and locked the yard door behind her, leaving me and the two remaining party guests outside.

"OI, OPEN UP THIS BLOODY DOOR!"

She came back a few moments later and we all heard the door unlock but she didn't come out, but instead turned round and walked off again.

This was the key low point where after this moment, a disastrous end to what should have been a great birthday celebration, I wanted to spend my remaining two days I had in this god forsaken city at the local airport instead. ANYWHERE but here. Not felt so despondent in another foreign city since staying in Potsdam, on the outskirts of Berlin a few years back previously with another mad Krautbitch whose name isn't even worth a pot to piss in. It was indeed a sombre time on my last day when I was driven to Dusseldorf Airport by Danie's mum and we were chatting half-heartedly about being born in the wrong era, Status Quo and hating chart music. At the airport we had some time to kill and I was kindly treated to a large dinner bought by Mum. Danie had perked up a little, too, and had at least the guts to actually apologize to me for being a bitch towards me, as she put it. But oh, how she surpassed herself in the realms of being a bitch, alright, because a week later and for the second time in my life, I found out that I was simply cast aside and dumped, via the internet.

And this was after she used to talk about living together and possibly having kids in the future.

Ho hum.

* * * * * * * *

AUGUST: MAD CORNISH MONSTER PSYCHO BITCH FROM THE 7 DEPTHS OF HELL
Chapter 1: Beginnings

I'd met Gill...later to be known as Mad Gill for obvious reasons...the very first time on a three day induction stint at St Loyes College in Exeter, Devon. She was alone smoking and the first thing I remember ever saying to her was "do you mind if I sit 'ere and smoke?" I'd been bollocked earlier by some jobsworth arsehole for attempting to have a fag in an apparently wrong section of a grassy area on the campus where there were benches situated and she was more than happy for a bit of company.

   She was of stocky build, short but thick curly chestnut coloured hair and had a thick Cornish accent. She was exactly one year and one month older than me and at this precise time in question I thought that all West Country accents sound pretty much the same, really (most people will obviously think that if you never been to this pretty region of England before), but Gill had an unsuspecting, almost childlike innocent charm that appealed to me but would later be my downfall. But then I oughta, shoulda realised that everyone that attended the college that I was referred to was a mature student suffering from some form of mental or physical disability and Gill was no exception. She was doing a catering course while I had just started a refresher course in Horticulture. While I had no real intention of forming any friendships with anyone, let alone bothering with a relationship with some wank girlfriend which was the last thing on my mind, I have been told that I'm a natural when it comes to making friends because I'm too easy going and too mild mannered. I'll chat to anyone who isn't ignorant but often enough this will occasionally turn into stuttering and it feels like I'm a gibbering idiot when it gets uncontrollable. But there you go-life isn't perfect, I'm not perfect and I try to get by without feeling too uncomfortable.

During the three day induction stint I was temporary settling down into Student Wanker life for the first time in 15 years. Me-a student-my GOD! And I've always hated students anyway. But it was during the induction that I had my first spliff party with some other new students. Well funny. I got pissed with Gill and it was her that popped the question and made no bones about it neither.

So I followed it up with the usual repertoire which oddly enough seems to work often:

"Well, d'ya fancy a snog then?"

And I got it, too. Well look, the way I see it is, why beat about the bush, if you don't ask, you don't get, innit!

Gill was quite drunk, and me being a gentleman and all, walked her back to her room in the woman's quarters. Of course, the Powers That Be had strict orders that male students weren't allowed into the women's quarters and vice versa but of course none of the students gave a shit about that and were completely oblivious to it. There were even stories that one or two of the students had at one point taken a couple of prozzies back to their digs. Get in!

At Gill's room we tried to have sex.
That is to say, I tried to have sex, but couldn't because I was so pissed I couldn't get an erection. So I got sucked off and I still couldn't get an erection. Floppy bloody thing! So we had a good old rummage about in her bed. Until about five minutes later, there was a sharp knock at the door.

Tap tap tap!

It was a female warden who could've passed for one of those hideously looking butch inmates out of Prisoner Cell Block H. She seemed butt ugly enough and grumpy enough to be one anyway but I acknowledged the fact that my chips were up and I was thinkin' that in no certain terms to get dress sharpish and get the hell out. But not before giving Gill a quick goodbye snog purposely in front of the warden which made her even more incensed. Heh! So while I was getting a bollocking of her/it while walking towards the exit/entrance of the ladies digs...and naturally ignoring her/it of course, although I could've turned round to wave a two finger salute at her/it...for one brief moment I thought about the future that lay ahead.

SEPTEMBER *Summer afternoon visits and fun at a garden centre*

I had quickly made friends with a great bloke on my course called Kieran who was in his early 20's and from King's Lynn, Cambridgeshire. He already had a fair knowledge of plants and plant care and his valuable tips and suggestions were often more helpful than the tutorage from my teachers themselves. As well as doing some college work, we had to do some work experience outside of St Loyes which was supposed to lead eventually to proper employment with an employer linked to the college as part of the work curriculum.

For me this came in the form of West Hill Garden Centre, a subsidiary of the much larger Otter Nurseries Ltd., a couple of miles down the road just outside the historic town of Ottery St Mary. Compared to Otter Nurseries, West Hill was tiny by comparison.

Getting to and from West Hill Garden Centre was difficult at first because the local buses leaving to and from Exeter Bus and Coach Station were limited to say the least; half the time the bus would leave from the wrong bay platform and would normally arrive and leave late; if you missed a bus it'd be a two hour wait for the next one so the bus I had to get to work had to be specific; and of course there are no bus stops on country lanes on rural routes so you had to be precise and tell the driver where you wanted to be dropped off.

Getting back from West Hill Garden Centre to campus digs was even more horrendous at the best of times; the nursery is situated just of a busy main road near a sharp bend so I was literally playing a game of human cat and mouse with the oncoming traffic once I left the nursery and the only safe place the bus would stop at was at a grassy verge next to a town destination board a few minutes' walk away.

It was also extremely important to leave a good ten minutes early than what the bus timetable specified because a lot of the time the bus would come unexpectedly early and I'd miss it, or on some occasions it didn't turn up at all, so I would have to troop back to Sally Manager and get a lift with her and her fella to a bus stop a couple or so of miles down the road in the opposite direction where there's a proper bus stop and shelter and this was served by a more regular bus service.

There were only three main staff working there, one part time. It was a joy working there because it felt more like best mates working together rather than a boss and her employee. Sally Manager and her assistant Kym and I struck up such a repertoire between us that half the time I didn't even feel like leaving the garden centre once I'd finished work: I'd already taken some interest in plants and horticulture having done a similar course some ten years earlier and it was fantastic having a brilliant working relationship with both people and learning different aspects of plants at the same time.

There was one funny incident one day when Sally and I hit upon the subject of shit James Bond films. That was a right giggle as it was but then the conversation changed from Bond films to cowboy films and then from cowboy films to John Wayne films and then further extended it yet from John Wayne films to John Wayne impersonations. This went on for something like a further three weeks until I unexpectedly got a full time job at Otter Nurseries. Life would never be the same after leaving West Hill because although I had been working on a voluntary basis, the respect, the humour, the fun and the laughs I had was a whole world away from what I was going to experience a couple of miles down the road.

* * * * * * * * * * *

   In the meantime, the friendship between me and Mad Gill was gradually flourishing. She'd always ask me if she could come to the shops or for a bevvy or three at the student bar. During what was known as 'non-warrant weekends' we'd go walking somewhere local or I'd take her out on a trip.
   On one of these trips I took her out to Dawlish Warren, about 10 miles down the road from Exeter. This should not be confused with Dawlish Town which is about another mile and a half up the coast, but according to various people 'not worth bothering about.' Now Dawlish Warren, that is nice. We travelled down there on the bus and during the trip my mobile rang.

   "Bollocks", I thought.
   It was Bobby the Beard. I tried to speak as quietly as possible to make myself discreet. But when I had to repeat the word 'Dawlish' three times, a chav couple sitting a few rows in front of us turned round to look at us, likewise a couple of half senile old bats did the same looking at me and muttered to themselves as if I was some alien from a distant planet.

"Did you see them two chav wankers looking at us?" I retorted indignantly to Gill, making sure they heard me. When the bus eventually arrived, we couldn't wait to get the fuck off and we headed towards the beach.
   It was still a mild and pleasant warm autumn atmosphere and the beach wasn't crowded. Wonderful, I thought. Gill went off for a dip and I settled down to improve my already brown skin on the sand and scoffed some food we bought with us. A couple nearby was listening to the cool sounds of ska and some alternative music which I could scarcely believe. I continued to bask out in the sun drinking cider and

when Gill came back from her dip in the ocean she couldn't believe I was still downing the equivalent of four pints of cider on a fairly hot day.

"Good thing I didn't have any cos me being as big as I am you might've had trouble carrying me home", she joked.

Gill never laughed, but she used to give out this odd sounding smirk if something amused her.
She also used to mumble constantly to herself whenever she was walking with me and often enough I'd stop and asked "Did you say summin?"

On another occasion, I took her to her very first ska gig at a large venue in Exeter city centre called The Phoenix to see a great Two Tone ska band called The Beat. The only original member of the band left is still 'Rankin Roger' still doing the business after all these years, and along with his son 'Rankin Junior' and new session members, this new version of The Beat are still the bollocks!

So there was I, wearing my pork pie hat and having a good old skank when a young woman comes up and starts to dance next to me. Nothing particularly unusual in that as this has happened a couple or so times when I've been to gigs. She spotted Gill who was nearby, turned her head round and in reference to her asked "Is that your girlfriend?"

"Yeah, that's right", I shouted back, trying to raise my voice above the din. She kissed me on the neck and slowly walked to Gill who was a few yards away and whispered in her ear: "I think your boyfriend's cute".

Being somewhat a naïve and sentimental idiot always did seem to be part of my unintentional forte because I had presumed that any other woman would've regarded that remark as a compliment, but all the poor woman got for her trouble was a violent shove from Gill that sent her sprawling to the ground. While momentary in shock she received an accusing finger from Gill who shouted out something I couldn't make out.

I looked at her, appalled.

"Why the bloody hell did you do that for?"

She didn't answer the question directly, but replied haughtily: "I'm going outside for a fag to calm down."

She stormed off. I picked the poor woman up from the floor and I couldn't have been more apologetic.

"You ok, luv? I really do apologize for that."

She was obviously a little shaken up, but otherwise, thankfully unhurt.

"Aren't you going to go after her?" she enquired.
"Wot, and miss the band playing? No chance. She'll 'ave to wait."

And indeed she did. In fact, when she came back a few minutes later looking somewhat flustered, I again tackled her about why she behaved liked that and her answer was quite blatant and flat.
"She was on drugs. She wasn't all there. She was definitely on something."

I sighed, and tried to think no more of the incident, although later on she revealed she was obviously jealous, but really I should've woken up to the fact that all this was a sure fire warning sign. I mean, the other day we had our first argument, in the student bar over whose turn was it to buy a fourth bottle of beer, and loudly complaining about it to the other students, for christ's sake.

* * * * * * *

MAD CORNISH MONSTER PSYCHO BITCH FROM THE 7 DEPTHS OF HELL
Chapter 2: Another gig experience for Gill

During the autumn I took Gill to another ska gig up town as she had enjoyed the first one I took her to. This time, to see an American skinhead rocksteady/reggae outfit called The Aggrolites. To tell the truth, they're not one of my favourite bands as Rocksteady is a form of ska I find too slow and boring, but it was a night out for Gill anyway. They were playing at a small venue called The Cavern which was modelled after its' more famous namesake in Liverpool. It was at this gig that I met for the first time a character who was to be in the future, a lifelong friend, a skinhead with an interesting moniker named after an animal, but for the purposes of this book, I'll simply refer to him as 'Dave'.

During the break we all went outside to have a fag and a natter. That is to say, Dave and Gill were chatting and I was having a stammering attack. Now, all stutterers are naturally shy people anyway, but the more I was trying to get the words out of my mouth, the worse the stammering got. I felt like a gibbering idiot about to get lockjaw but Gill put a reassuring hand on my arm and gently squeezed.

That squeeze felt like the best thing in the world at that precise moment: despite all of Gill's faults, she could be the most wonderful, sincere and kindest person in the world and it was one of those treasured moments like this that I wouldn't forget for a long time.

After the gig had finished we all trooped back to Dave's place to continue the piss up. Still being fairly new to Exeter, we didn't know how to get back to the college which was approximately one and a half miles away. We ordered a taxi but none showed up after waiting for 30 minutes so we decided to walk it, Dave giving us directions and constantly reassuring us that it would only be a "ten minute walk."

Ten minutes' walk, my brown arse. What should've been a brisk thirty minutes' walk turned into a nightmare fifty minute crawl as of course we were completely bolloxed and we were walking slowly; plus we took a wrong turn unfortunately and were temporary lost. By the time we did get back to the college campus we were totally exhausted and footsore; Gill suddenly stopped dead still and gave me a confused and embarrassed glance: she had literally shat her trousers.

LATE AUTUMN *Hatred of Roz "Mrs. Hitler" Tyrant*

I woke a few hours later and went to work with a hangover. The workplace, which I had been there barely a fortnight which had led almost directly from work experience at the nearby West Hill Garden Centre a couple of miles up the road, was at a far larger garden centre called Otter Nurseries, the premier centre for gardening tools, equipment...and a whole variety of plants, shrubs and small trees...in the entire South West. The place was so big it even had its' own restaurant and that coachloads of tourists (mainly elderly) come regularly.

I was working as a garden nursery assistant assigned to the habaetious section working with a tyrant of a supervisor called Roz and doing mainly cultivating. Before getting a full time job here- BADLY paid full time job here by the way as I was on a basic minimum wage of a paltry £5.52 an hour and no one can survive on a pathetic wage like that in this country these days- I was a lot more happier working with Sally Manager and Kym for nothing.

I was working with some middle aged lads whose name escapes me, but one originally hailed from Sevenoaks, in Kent. Another was a local man that supported Man. City (I asked him about this once, that it made a bloody big change he supported the other 'big' Manchester club as opposed to all these glory hunting countryside wankers that supported Man. Urinal and I think his reply was something to do with Mike Summerbee and Denis Law sending the Red Scum down into what was then the old Second Division in the mid Seventies, hahahaha!)

I was also working with some young Polish lads who hated Roz with a vengeance. She had barked at them once when they were quietly talking amongst themselves in Polish, saying "only speak English". I supposed she had a point but she needn't have had been so fucking rude about it.

Roz was universally hated by just about everyone. She may have been an exceptional person who excelled in horticulture and knew her stuff inside out but she was at the bottom of the class when it came to people and social skills. She was fat and pudgy with a double chin, had short but stringy dark hair, butt ugly, always scowled and shuffled from side to side when she walked. It was rare she ever smiled, let alone laughed because she did herself no favours by treating most of the staff like shit and ran her horticultural section like it was a car production line. It was pretty relentless.

After a few days of working with her, the Man. City fan said: "What do you think of 'Mother'?" ('Mother' being the somewhat unsympathetic nickname for Roz.)
"Do you really want to know?" I replied sullenly.
He nodded, waiting for the answer.
"I think she's the most rudest, most vilest person I've ever had to work under and I dunno how she gets away with talking and treating people like that."
"Yep- that's 'Mother' for you", he continued with countenance. "Bear with her during your trial period. Keep your head down. Try not to let her get to you. After your trial period's up, and you're made permanent staff, you can put in an official complaint about her."

* * * * * * *

OCTOBER *The first real taste of the extreme South West*

Everything I was told about the West Country, and later on to my utter regret and disgust, further west into Cornwall, seemed to have been mostly justified in terms of sheer ignorance. There's a saying that anywhere you go, you'll meet arseholes, that's just a fact of life, and different areas of Britain have different levels of ignorance. None so more than Devon and Cornwall, which makes ignorance in London seem almost transparent. Exeter is a small city, with small mindedness from ignorant morons and here are three examples of this, the first one actually coming from a teacher at St Loyes, who was later to become a firm acquaintance who I'd see down at the terraces at St James' Park watching Exeter City play:

"Why are you dressed like that? I thought all skinheads were white."
"Just goes to show how much you know about skinheads then, don't it? And anyway, why are you bothered about how I look? I mean, how would you like it if I had a pop at you about how *you* dressed?"

The second example came from some brain dead redneck at St David's Station; with the same question but with a personal touch added when he said, highly originally, that I was black.
Get away, I thought. Ten outta ten for observation, you thick Devon twat.

"Is that so?" I began. "Well tell me, isn't that a bit like saying how come there's so many white people that are into crap like R'n'B and Gangster Rap?"

The thick bastard actually thought about this momentarily before murmuring "oh yeah", by which then I'd walked off giving him the finger salute while he trying to defend himself by saying he wasn't racist.

The third, and probably the most extreme example was when I was walking in the St James' Park area of Exeter and an elderly lady actually crossed the road to the other side where I was just to ask, "So which part of Africa do you come from?"

"Which part of Poland do YOU come from?" I immediately replied back.

The ignorant old bat was completely taken by surprise when I said this and before she had a chance to reply I cut in, "you Hungarian? Lithuanian? No? Slovakian?"

She stuttered out "No, Yorkshire-"but before she had a chance to finish her sentence, I spat out "Right, well why don't you fuck off back there then," before storming off and leaving the lady utterly shell-shocked.

MAD CORNISH MONSTER PSYCHO BITCH FROM THE 7 DEPTHS OF HELL
Chapter 3: Behavioural problems

The first real sign that Mad Gill had some sort of behavioural disorder problem started shortly after I had just left St David's Station one night and got a bus back into town, I phoned Gill, but her tone was stone cold. Something was up and I didn't know what had happened, so I was left mystified. I got back to college and the insults started. Not verbally face to face but by text. I'd never had a slanging match by mobile texting before so this was something very new, very different and decidedly very nasty.

This carried on the next morning when I was at work at Otter Nurseries. I was getting bloody sick of all this and after work I got off at my usual bus stop and walk the mile back to campus down Burnthouse Lane, a supposedly notorious no-go chav area (I myself never got any hassle apart from one time when I was talking to a friend on my mobile while sitting on a wall and a snooty nose Asian woman walking past but looking down at me as if I was dirt, to which she received a "what the fuck are you looking at", before continuing on.) Even so, I was always wary and alert just in case it did kick off.

As I was approaching the college down the lane, Mad Gill was walking towards some local shops accompanied by another mature student acquaintance called Anthony. I couldn't even bear to look Gill in the face as I was too enraged (and I didn't want to make a public scene with Anthony involved.) She walked off to a nearby convenience store and Anthony noticed my strained look on my face.

"You ok, Mick?" he asked.
"Not really. Gill's been treating me like some cunt by accusing me of sleeping around."

Anthony looked emotionless, but he was clearly disgusted.

"You don't need that sort of shit, especially after a hard day at work."

I nodded and carried on walking towards the college, alone.
Later on, I had a word with a good friend called Kane, another mature student. Kane was one really genuine funny bloke who has had his fair share of life's misfortunes and illnesses but nothing seemed to have gotten him down despite what he has been through and he always had a cheerful smile on his face. He once made a true life event joke about rural pubbing culture in Dorset which he actually experienced and this just about summed up rural pubbing culture in Devon and Cornwall:

"I ordered a pint of Fosters and sat down near the corner of the pub. A local shouted out that he couldn't sit there as it was 'Bill's seat, and only Bill sits at that chair'. But a moment ago you mentioned that Bill was dead. Yes, I know he's dead, he carried on, but that's still Bill's seat!"

I explained the situation about myself and Gill and he began to look a little sheepish. He was even more embarrassed when I showed him some of the filthy texts Gill had sent.

"I'm afraid that's partly to do with me," he started to explain.
"Hmm? How do you mean?" I enquired.
"I mentioned to Gill that as you're a popular guy, you should have a fan club. I think she took it the wrong way and thought you had a sexual fan club."
"Sexual fan cl-" I broke off and rolled my eyes. "Oh for fuck's sake..."
"Look, we'll be leaving soon." (The college was due to close for the usual bank holiday bollocks.) "Don't end this on a sour note. Talk to her and explain things out."

At least Kane had been decent enough to have the guts to own up to the fact it was indirectly his fault for this whole mess but it also took more guts for me to try to calm Gill down especially as the abusive texts were still flying thick and fast, but then they suddenly stopped abruptly when I texted her: "Gill, we need to talk. Don't let it end like this."

THE WINTER OF RACIAL DISCONTENT

The winter of 2007 was going to end disastrously, like the previous year before and all other previous years before that, too. But 2007 was going to lead into an even more horrible new year which no one could've ever foreseen. How could I have predicted this when thing were in general, going fairly well? I had a paid job for the first time in five years, I had a girlfriend, I was living outside London which I always wanted and had made new friends. So wot went wrong?

Here were the events that led up to it.

A couple of weeks into November, the manager of St Loyes said I'd have to find another place as I was no longer officially recognised as a mature student anymore now that I was working full time. And this was after the college kept on encouraging me and the other students to actively seek work while studying in the first place. No mention of trying to help you find digs once you get a job locally in the Exeter and the surrounding districts whatsoever. Bit hypercritical if you ask me, but there you go.

At work however, it became more beneficial to work far quicker and easier without the hindrance of 'Mrs. Hitler' as she had now become known, as she'd often leave the workplace to attend to other matters elsewhere around the garden centre by travelling around on a small tractor. Good bloody riddance. I secretly fantasied about her crashing into a ditch somewhere and she was stuck getting out, breaking both legs. The Polish lads also had a special word for her which I couldn't pronounce.

We were all working one day getting stuck in as usual when she suddenly upped and left without a word and didn't come back. She had to attend a meeting but had decided not to tell any of us. (Well, she didn't tell me or the Polish lads anyway.)

I was told later on that she often does this but me being the New Kid on the Block I wouldn't have known about it, so I made the crass mistake of politely enquiring how she was the next morning as I was actually genuinely concerned about her.

She barked out a haughty laugh which sounded more like a suppressed dry cough.

"Look", she started, in that horrible sarky drone of hers, and carried on somewhat imposingly: "I am the team manager of this section here. Where I go is *my* concern and I don't have to tell *you* my business where *I* go."

I looked at her, quite astounded by her reaction, but once again decided to button my lip and keep quiet. From that moment onwards I lost all respect for her not just as a manageress, but as a person, too.

One day while we had our usual half hour break for lunch in the canteen, Sally from West Hill called on my mobile to discuss about various herbs and plants. It was all I could do to stop myself from bursting into fits of laughter as the conversation became as humourous as ever. I turned my head slightly and out of the corner of my eye was Roz the Tyrant glaring at me. I mean, proper evils. That was enough to give anyone the shits with the utter look of contempt Roz had just giving me and I never bothered to have lunch in the canteen room ever again.

I then decided to spend all my free time with a unique motley crew of various workers from the different parts of the vast garden centre simply known to everyone else as the 'Smoking Gang' where we'd all meet up at a designated smoking area in the guise of a large bus shelter (later, that was demolished and a gazebo was built next to the canteen. The only problem with that was that to enter it you had to go into the canteen first and go on through the back.)

It was here that I met up with a person called Ronnie (from the East Enders character) because she had a ice cool attitude about her and rarely smiled but she was very intelligent and was bi-lingual (she spoke fluent Spanish). She had a job as an advisor on various plants, herbs, soil and just about anything and everything else to do with horticulture. We struck up a friendship and eventually agreed to car share as it would work out financially cheaper between us (beats having to rely on a rubbish and expensive bus service all the time.)

She also had a helping hand in finding me an alternative place to live as time was running out fast at the college and it was getting closer to Christmas. The place she suggested was far from ideal as it was a small room in a shared house 15 minutes out of the city centre and ideally a few minutes' walk from St James' Park football ground. I was dead against having to house share with a set of people I have absolutely nothing in common with for the fourth time in my life, but all else had failed, so I didn't have much choice. No matter how many times I looked up various websites, looked in various newspapers and shop windows, the result was always the same. "Sorry, the place has already gone", or in some cases not even a reply at all.

There were even two cases where I was the first person to view a property to rent but yet was told the property had gone to someone else.

I was now beginning to think Exeter must still be stuck in an early Sixties time warp with 'Windrush' and doors advertising "No Irish, No Blacks and No Dogs" like it was in London at the time. I'm not one to use the so-called 'race card' scenario crap but I can't help thinking that institutionalized racism is rife as fuck around here.

DECEMBER

"How to use a broom properly" by Roz the Tyrant, in several volumes, published only at Otter Nurseries, Ottery St Mary, Devon, Redneckshire.

Roz "Mrs. Hitler" was doing her best to wind me up more and more and the more I refused to give in to her, the more it seemed her anger towards me grew. She was deliberately causing a foment with me and the Polish lads, but I'll be damned if an ignorant lump like her was going to get the better of me. The days were growing colder and colder and there was no proper wall or ceiling in the true sense to protect us from the biting winds. I unfortunately suffer from low blood circulation in my hands so my hands are always cold anyway, but during the winter it's a real problem and my fingers will literally turn blue so I have to constantly rub my hands or put my hands into my pockets often for the heat to return to my hands. Gloves, also I found wasn't the best thing when cultivating certain shrubs and flowers so it was always done with your bare hands, so although I was doing as much work as everyone else, it was slower. Roz saw this and barked out at me to work faster.

"I cannot. I have to stop every now and again to rub my hands. Low blood circulation problems."
Roz exploded. "Did you not put that on your application form before you started working here full time?"
"No, I don't think I did."
"I'll have to report this to my manager," she said, almost with a bit of sarcastic glee.
I looked up at her and shrugged.
"Well", I began tactfully, "Do what you must do, Roz."

I continued with my work. Roz stormed off. But when she came back a little while later she looked as if she was about to burst a blood vessel. Obviously her threat had backfired and she'd come out second best. I glanced at her, and continued with my work with a wry smile to myself.
Towards the end of December all the various garden departments were to have a special Christmas dinner amongst their staff; but the dinner was no different to what was being cooked this month, or any other month for that matter. AND we had to pay extra, the tight bastards. The thought of having to sit at the same table as Roz the Tyrant or even being within two yards of her was foreboding indeed. Especially when awhile back I'd got a bollocking for using a broom "the wrong way" (she had observed me using it casually with one hand while my other hand was in my pocket. She actually stormed over to where I was, grabbed the broom handle out of my hand and demonstrated...yes, demonstrated..."how to use a broom properly with two hands" savagely sweeping some rubbish into a small pile.
I stared at her quite aghast and for a split moment decided to either burst out laughing in hysterics or say something rude and sarky. I did neither. It just wasn't worth wasting my breath. Her action what she did wasn't just downright sarcastic, it was downright pathetic. I dunno if she was trying to belittle me by acting like a pompous twat but she

sure as hell wasn't doing a particularly good job of it, the patronizing bitch.

At the Christmas dinner, I was rapidly beginning to get bored with all this waiting. Extremely bored. There seem to be some delay with the dinner being served so I quite blatantly got up and left to go to the gazebo to have a fag with the Smoking Gang. A few minutes later when I had returned and dinner still hadn't been served so I began to make polite but idle chit chat with one of the Polish lads. Personally I couldn't wait for this farce of a festive Christmas dinner to be over.
   A few days later the entire garden centre closed down for a two week Christmas break.

Good riddance.

MAD CORNISH MONSTER PSYCHO BITCH FROM THE 7 DEPTHS OF HELL *Chapter Four:*
Mad Cornish Monster Psycho Bitch from the 7 Depths of Hell shows her true colours

   I went back to London with Gill to spend some time quality Christmas time with Mum and then on Boxing Day got the National Express coach back to Penzance, a nine hour nightmare journey. My crappy suitcase was giving me jip and playing silly buggers as it seemed to have a mind of its own as I was dragging the fucker by its strap and it kept on swaying to one side and then to the other and toppling over.
   We decided to celebrate the new year by going to one of Mad Gill's three older sisters, Heather, who looks a lot older than she should be and is softly spoken, lives in what I would call TRUE utopia, a coastal village called Sennen Cove, a mile from Lands' End.
   All the houses are named, not numbered, and all of them are situated on steep hills overlooking the Atlantic Ocean. To say that the

view here was breath taking and stunning was an understatement. During the day Gill took me to Lands' End via a 'petrified forest.' For you history buffs out there, a petrified forest isn't a forest that you and I might think off: just loads of, well, uneven rocks, really. She also showed me the remains of what once a castle. Or an abbey. Or wotever the fuck it was supposed to be because absolutely nothing remains of wotever building it was supposed to be but a clump of large rocks barely distinguishable from all the other rocks and rubble scattered across the windswept landscape.

We continued further and passed a couple of tourists, one of them a poxy West Ham dickhead who was wearing a ghastly bubble-hat who stared at me as if I was from outer space.

"What's that West Ham cunt gawping at?" I said aloud as I stared back at him. "Twat!"

We reached Lands' End.

This was the first ever time I've been here and I wasn't impressed.

"Is this it?" I looked at Gill blankly. "Not much cop this, innit!"

I dunno wot all the fuss about Lands' End is really, and why it attracts so many stupid wanky tourists. We're at the very edge of Britain, and all there is, is a large hotel, some amusement arcades...and, er, that's basically it. One big yawn.

Sennen Cove, about a mile back to the east, has a genuinely better view. And no stupid wanky tourists polluting the area neither.

Later on that night, after a mouth-watering pheasant dinner prepared and cooked by Heather, we decided to pop down to a local pub to see in the New Year. It was a strangely warm night when it should've been freezing so we didn't bother wearing jumpers or pullovers. We entered the pub and I started chatting to a young barman who liked my clobber I was wearing and commented that he

wouldn't have had the nerve to wear a Fred Perry or Harrington jacket as people would get the wrong idea about him; a misconception that I frequently get.
 I shrugged and smiled at him.

 "Ah, but you shouldn't worry about wot other people think of yer. Be yerself and fuck the rest!"

And for that remark I got a free bottle of Budweiser.

Result, or wot!

 Now for most of this time, Gill had been drinking by herself and Heather and her boyfriend Andy had been chatting amongst themselves. I realised too late yet again that the more Gill drank, the more her frustration and rage was beginning to boil inside her.
 I had started to mingle with some of the locals who all knew Gill, particularly one couple I had made the mistake of being acquainted with.

 "I hear it's very hot this time of year in Ghana."

 I frowned at him, but ignored what he had just blurted out and carried on drinking.
 When this ignorant dumbfuck said more or less the same thing again a few minutes later, the anger began to boil inside me but still I kept quiet and carried on drinking.
 His missus then spoke. It was the dreaded question I absolutely loathed being asked.

 "Where do you come from? Are you from Africa?"
That was it. This was one of the rare occasions where I finally lost my temper and I let of real steam.
 "Right, so where do YOU come from?"

Dumbfuck Bitch mentioned some Northern town but I was too enraged to acknowledge or registered the fact she'd even said it, and I cut in sharply.

"So yer quite sure you ain't Polish? Or from some other poxy Eastern European country?"

Before she had a chance to reply, I told her to fuck off.

   I was literally about to explode so I went outside to the beer garden into the cool night air to calm down.
I went back inside a few minutes later to find Gill 'minesweeping' (a South Western term used to describe someone nicking someone else's drinks as many times as possible) and was practically falling over the gaff. There is some unwritten rule that when you see a bloke pissed and acting like a twat that's bad enough, but when a bird is pissed and acting like a twat, it's more than just embarrassing.
   I was downing my seventh bottle of Bud when Heather and Andy decided to call it a day...or in this case, night, to head of back home. Luckily it was only a short walk but Mad Gill had become paralytic and was hurling insults at me left right and centre. I'd never seen a grown woman drool saliva before, but it was a bloody frightening sight seeing and hearing Mad Gill in such a state. I took one more insult from her and shouted at her to fuck off.
   Before she had a chance to reply back, Andy pushed her to the ground. She really did look quite pathetic in a heap like that. She got up after a few seconds and carried on walking behind us still shouting but her words becoming more unintelligible. We eventually got back to Heather's house, a little worse for the wear.

   For a split second- a nano second even- I visualised this scenario reminiscent of one of them Hollywood fantasy 'blockbusters' where time stands still for a second where everything else in reality flies by: Mad Gill had swung a left hook and punched me on the right side of my face. That punch should've left me reeling as it was like the power of a pile driver and I certainly felt its impact. The pain didn't register because I was drunk. When a person is drunk, you don't normally register acute pain when you're hurt physically (would explain why there is so much aggro at pubs and gigs.)

   Andy then rugby tackled her to the ground and tried to pin her there, but the frightening image I'll always remember is that she was still struggling frantically to get up to attack me even though she received a couple of slaps from him.

   I looked at them blankly but half dazed and then turned to Heather who, herself was in a confused state, trying to comprehend the scene she was witnessing. I went into her house to crash out on a prepared spare bed on the dining room floor she had kindly made up for me earlier and tumbled onto it half unconscious and tried to get some kip while I left the three of them to it in the commotion still raging outside.

   During the night however, after things had finally settled down or so I thought, things took a more sinister turn as Mad Gill kept on popping into the dining room to get a glass of water while at the same time having a verbal pop at me. This continued for some time and then during yet another impromptu visit she savagely threw a cosmetics bag I had given to her for a Christmas present at me to which I replied drowsily: "Bitch."

   Throughout the remainder of what was left of the night I was constantly worrying and fretting about what else she might do to me while half dozing off and waking up again and when early morning dawn arrived a couple of hours later, the most oddest thing about Mad Gill occurred.

   From her warped point of view it appeared that all traces of the incident a few hours earlier was like some distant memory or indeed that the incident never actually happened at all as she calmly walked into the dining room where I was still half dozing and cheerfully asked me if I wanted a cup of tea.

I looked at her for a few seconds, somewhat incredulously, trying to grasp the situation before I answered her question.
"Well yeah, alright then, if yer making a brew."

Welcome to 2008.

"What a wonderful, marvellous start to the new year." I thought to myself sarcastically.

       *   *   *   *   *   *   *

PART TWO

2008 *A geezer worse than Roz*

Where do I start?

When I returned back to work after the Christmas and New Year break, I was transferred to another section at Otter Nurseries to work with an utter bastard of a guy, a lanky streak of piss who I shall name Jobsworth who was even more horrendous to work with than Roz and had one of the strangest West Country accents ever. Someone actually *worse* than Roz?? Not possible, surely, you ask. You'd better believe it. If there was ever a cunt that was known for 'double standards' with certain people, he was top of the class. He was loathed by many people who worked at the nursery including many of the men that had to work under him.

His whole, entire, pathetic life revolved around his work and the workplace and many people suspected he didn't have any sort of social life outside work at all. His section was split into two quarters, the women's and the men's. The women could do no wrong in his eyes, gossiping bunch of muppets, the lot of them. They reminded me of another bunch of gossiping idiots, the women who worked in Mike Baldwin's factory out of *Coronation Street*.
   Once, I had to work outside with a work colleague to cultivate some shrubs, but they had be done in a certain way where you couldn't sit so you had to squat. Jobsworth demonstrated to us once how it should be done properly then went off somewhere. The situation he left us in made work extremely difficult squatting like this and I was beginning to get cramp after barely five minutes, and it was not a warm day, adding more misery.

   The best way I found to complete the work set was to cultivate, stand up and stretch and then cultivate every few minutes. Jobsworth came back from wherever he went, saw me, but didn't go directly to where I was, but shouted at me to get to where he was standing a few yards away.

"What do you think you're doing? Get on with your work and do it quicker like I showed you," he bellowed.
"Do it quicker?? Well, why don't you *demonstrate* to me again how to do it quicker then?"
"Don't you *tell* me how to do my job, I'm the manager and you're not, do you understand?"

   Oh, I fuckin' understand, alright. Understand that if he talked down at me one more time, he'd get a well- deserved smack.

   He walked off. Unbeknown to him however, his rant had been heard by a workman in another section of the centre nearby and came up to speak to me.

"Who the fuck does he think he is, talking to people like that?"
"That bloke is an utter cunt. He talks down to people all the time. I'm surprised he's not been punched by someone yet."

I couldn't wait to get home that evening and it took me most of the night to recover from stiff legs and cramp.

I had a bit of welcome relief when I had to work in a sub-section of his area with other workers, yet again divided into men's and women's departments. Now at this particular time in England, the first wave of Polish workers were flooding into the country, causing a lot of resentment for many people. I wasn't bothered about talk about how they are such hard working people. I wasn't bothered about talk about how apparently most of them live four to a room in a house to save money for themselves. I wasn't even too bothered about talk about how no English person would apparently do menial jobs like fruit picking, cleaning jobs and the like so therefore various companies would employ cheap Polish labour and saving themselves a fortune by NOT hiring British people. What I WAS bothered about was just how fucking pig ignorant and up their own arse the majority of these people were, as if they all had a personal invitation by the Queen herself and strutting around as if they own the gaff.

When one of the female workers asked the dreaded question "Are you from Africa", I responded immediately, "Why is it that people like you automatically think that all black people have to come from fucking Africa?"

"I'm sorry," she said, startled. "I thought-"

"That's just it, you DIDN'T think, did you? I mean, how would you like it if every arsehole asked you 'where do you come from?' Soppy cow!"

This wasn't the first time I had been subjected to the same old bloody question at Otter Nurseries.
In fact it was the third. In fact, this irritating line of questioning was beginning to be so frequent I really did thought it was an ignorant thick

West Country thing where the only time anyone happened to see a person that was black, brown or otherwise was on television.

And all happening to come from Africa, naturally.

The first time it happened was when I was with the Smoking Gang and a well-meaning, but somewhat dim witted cashier assistant from Honiton had popped the question.

"You wot?" I asked, as I inhaled. "What makes you say that?"
"Well, where do your parents come from?"
"London, where I was born. That good enough for you?"
"So where were your parents born?"
"Jamaica, if you must know," I carried in impatiently.
"I reckon you'd look good in them plats and braids. My friend does her hair like that."
"Are you taking the piss now?"

Honiton, a large market town 16 miles east of Exeter, was one of the places I went to, to view a flat above a shop. One look at me and the landlord said he had given the flat to someone else. Honiton, as you gathered, is one of the most horrible, redneck towns alive. Anyone who is a shade of brown are apparently all of-shoots of Kunta Kinte, the slave bloke outta 'Roots'. So it didn't surprise me that she was waffling on like that.

Most of the male workers were great to work with, and there was one memorable moment when two of them got into a friendly argument about the existence of life and every time one of them said a question, the other one would counter-argue with another question.

"Well, why is grass called grass then?"
"Bollocks to that, who was it that invented the word 'grass'? I mean it must've been someone who had a bright idea of writing down the

word 'grass', might've well could've just wrote down the word 'arse' and describe it as what cows and sheep eat, ain't it!"

FEBRUARY *The Gay Capital of Devon and the eventual sacking*

If Brighton in Sussex is supposedly the gay capital of England, then Exeter is surely the queer capital of the South West. One of the housemates in the house I had to share, affectionately known as "Gay Steve" was more camp than Larry Grayson and Liberace put together and while I personally have nothing against gays in general he was getting very close to getting smacked over having to hear his endless tales of his love life with various partners in that horrible feminine voice of his.

Among the other housemates which I also had absolutely nothing in common with was a 40 year old meathead living with an obese teenager from nearby Crediton who would always waffle on about fighting and "being hard" (yaaaawn), yet another idiot who loved dishing it out verbally but couldn't take it back. When he had racially insulted me as a "joke", this is what I said as a reply.

"Watch your mouth, farmboy."

Did he *not* like *that*.

The last of the housemates were a young female and her drug dealing scum of a fella who would use the house as a means of an operation base but not actually live there. I pissed him off once and received a hiding which included a fractured nose, but I'd done the trick as he'd ran off and there was no loud music playing for the first time in ages.

From then on, things began to rapidly slide downhill. Jobsworth was even more unbearable to work with when he found fault when I had to pluck the dead leaves of trays of pansies and made me look a cunt slagging me off in front of everyone even though I was doing just as much work as everyone else, and more in the case of the women's section who were working slightly slower but of course they could do no wrong with Jobsworth.

I was near exploding point and when he eventually left I banged on the table so hard the entire section of where I was, rattled. The women glanced at each other but didn't say anything.

I knew the end for me was gathering momentum. Jobsworth came back about half an hour later, called me over and marched me straight to the manager's office. A few words were said and I was dismissed. Exactly three months after I had started, a remarkable coincidence.

The last words he said to me was, "when you drop by, perhaps you can drop of the jacket."

How I wished I'd turned round to punch him in the mouth then and there. But I had my dignity to uphold and I carried on walking as if I hadn't heard him and out of Otter Nurseries forever.

The way I saw myself wasting my life for three months at Otter Nurseries was a bit like this: I was the only non-white person working in the entire centre there and my cards were marked from the second I started working for Otter. They saw me as just cheap casual labour on a trial period for minimum wage and once the three months were up I was gotten rid of. It made more sense to the company to do this on a regular basis than hire people full time, apart from the Polish who would "work three times as hard for the same amount of money." One of them didn't even speak English so I once asked Roz when she was in one of her better moods how is it that Otter employed someone that couldn't understand English. I mean, how did the bloke fill in the application form, for example?

I went to Citizen's Advice to see if it was possible to sue Otter for unfair dismissal, but I didn't stand a chance. According to some bullshit law, a person would have had to work 6 months to a year to claim and any time before that a company could do pretty much anything to a worker. Otter knew what they were doing, alright. It's called exploitation and to say I felt hard done by was an understatement.

Having gotten drunk with Dave the skinhead that night, I now had to weigh the pros and cons of my situation. I now had no job so now I couldn't pay the rent although I despised living there. I still had my flat in Beckenham but I didn't like London either. I had to swallow my pride and admit that things weren't working out in the West Country financially. I had the offer of temporary living at another friends' flat, but that would be just it: temporary and it would mean having once again to share with people. I needed my independence and I needed it fast.

So back to London I had to go, but within a year I would be back.

And it turned out to be the biggest mistake I ever regretted.

*   *   *   *   *   *   *

PART THREE:
2009: The Great Escape (from London)

JANUARY *"I don't understand the human race. That's why I can't relate to people."*

Britain emerged spitting from the arse end of one of the worse years in living memory for the majority of people, straight into a European recession which Britain itself had ironically started just after last year's autumn. The country now was going through its worse economic meltdown since the early 1970's with businesses and pubs being closed down at the rate of five per day somewhere in Britain; millions forced to go on the dole but at the same time mass immigration into England from the African continent and Eastern Europe, the principal country being Poland (if you're likely to believe even established newspapers like the upper crust Times or even The Guardian frequently screaming out headlines like "POLISH IMMIGRANTS TAKE OVER JOBS" or "120 LANGUAGES SPOKEN AT PRIMARY SCHOOL" which up to a few years ago would've been exclusively said by trash like The Sun then you know there has to be some amount of truth in what you are reading and not just sensationalism, and believe me I've seen it and everyone else has for themselves.

It makes me laugh when the only people who actually embrace this are mummy's boys and mummy's girls Student Wankers and the well-off who have no idea what the real world is like; never known what it's like to be homeless, or manage to scrape a meagre living on pittance or have to wait years for a crap council place on some run-down estate and are ready to cite 'racist' when 'immigration' is spoken, an almost taboo subject these days. Over the course of a couple of years, whole suburbs, towns and even most cities have changed forever.

I was sick of London.

I was sick to death of this poxy, fucked up city for years.

I was sick of my neighbours, especially that po-faced bitch from next door who had put up a fence separating my balcony from hers.

I was sick of my tiny one bedroom flat which was purposely designed in such a stupid way that for me or anyone else to use the bathroom, they would have to go through my bedroom.

I was sick of having to cope with travelling on over-crowded local buses and trains full to the brim with loud mouth Africans and Polish shouting loudly into their poxy mobile phones constantly and persistently as they were boldly trying (and succeeding) of making a point to other people of their presence.

I was sick of two faced, so-called 'friends' constantly letting me down.

I was sick of the claustrophobia, the pollution.

I was sick of graffiti everywhere, the stench, the smell.

In fact, I was sick to death of everything and anything to do with London.

Football, which was once my escapism from a mundane, dull life was frequently taking a back seat as it was no longer affordable, and the whole punk thing for me was practically non-existent these days. I had grown tired of punk, with its bullshit ultra-political correctness and double standards, and had turned to the somewhat more extreme, if you want to label it that way, skinhead movement. Thing is though, I never regarded myself as being in ANY movement; I just chose to look skinhead, or 'Rude Boy'.

Skinheads, as a whole had always been labelled by the media and GPS (general public scum) as all nationalistic racist thugs which is an interesting theory seeing that there are just as many racist trendies, rockabillies, gays,, blacks, Asians- in fact all people from all walks of life.

But why *especially* skinheads?

It could be the fact that the majority of skinheads are patriotic which personally I do not see it as a problem. Many people seem to think there is an extremely fine line between patriotism and blatant racism but there is a *whole* load of difference between patriotism and blatant racism as I've always argued the point that you can have a love for anything- football club, country, whatever-and not be a Nazi twat about it.

Take for example, Cornwall. Most Cornish people are fiercely independent and rightly quite proud of being Cornish but don't consider themselves being English or even acknowledge the fact of Cornwall being even remotely part of England. It has its' own national flag and language which is similar to Welsh but in all reality that language is practically dead as hardly anyone speaks it anymore and it exists only on the majority of road and street names and on certain buildings, particularly in West Cornwall.

Are they considered racist?

I'll let you be the judge of that once you finish reading this book.

Also, take for example Ireland, where for some inexplicable reason which I could never understand personally, the whole western world turn into pretend Irishmen to celebrate St Patrick's Day (it makes me want to vomit when some dumb Yank waffle on about their "Oirish-American heritage" while at the same time doing their bit for Uncle Bloody Sam pledging their allegiance to the American flag (I wonder what reaction we'd all have if we pledged allegiance to the flag of St George or the Union Jack. Oh, I forgot, we can't do that over here can we cos then we'd all be considered racist. Sorry.) and then go thousands of miles to bomb the fuck outta countries like Iraq ("I-Rawhk as our American friends like to imply) in their never-ending quest for "truth, justice and the American way".

And oil.

Watch any Michael Moore film documentary or the puppet film "Team America: World Police" one day and then you'll know what I'm on about. A savage satirical swipe on what most people thinks wot America is all about. Hypercritical. And that leads straight onto the real start of Part Three.

The Final Goodbyes

During January, I was corresponding with Mad Gill, now an ex as I finally saw sense to dump, but were still loosely on talking terms. I was so desperate to escape life in London, we were talking about the possibility of me moving into her flat temporary before finding digs of my own and a job as soon as possible. She was renting a flat in one of the most remote towns in Cornwall, St Just, one mile from the edge of Britain facing the Atlantic Coast.

We came to an amicable agreement that I could indeed stay for a bit; and so for the next three weeks I was shifting most of my belongings from my flat bit by bit as I couldn't afford a removal van (it must've been a right sight with the snoopy neighbours and every other bloody local watching me lug a great big red suitcase and a large bag once or twice a day to the local railway station, getting a train to mum's a few miles away in Herne Hill, dumping the stuff and then back to my shitty, grubby flat in Beckenham again.)

While all this was going on, I was trying to visit as many friends as possible, a foolhardy event I was soon made to regret.

This included a trip to East Anglia to visit two friends; an acquaintance called Taz from Colchester and long-time soul mate Chrissy from 'nearby' Stowmarket. Chrissy is one of these people that would never in the whole world bother to get of her arse to visit me at all (I think she only ever came round to visit me two or three times in thirteen years when she still lived in South London) but yet would expect me to drop everything to visit her. On the day in question, it was a cold, miserable Sunday and absolutely pissing down with rain and I was thinking why the fuck am I bothering with all this.

Because I'm a man of my word and will think of others before rather than myself-another trait that I have long lived to regret also.

I've not seen Taz in two years and had lost touch until recently. So it was good to hook up with her again.
I met her outside Colchester Town station shivering my arse off in the cold when she drove up, picked me up and then drove to her house and met her old man. I dumped my stuff then went to a local pub together where I had some lunch. I offered to pay but she was having none of it, so I paid for a few beers.

Colchester is a squaddie town with a crap football team. It may be a town steep in history (Colchester is recorded as the oldest inhabited town in England, and its' first capital) but it's still full of wankers. I said my goodbyes and travelled up to Stowmarket by train, for which I was not best pleased of paying a score for a "cheap day return", and that's after I bunked halfway up there too.

After meeting up with Chrissy, looking very chic and trendy (that's Chrissy for you-she was always one for style and taste and she looked great in anything she wore) we went on a booze session via a couple of local pubs, met some of the locals, one a right total yokel who I don't think had ever saw a black person in his life, the way the poor bastard kept on staring, but then, where we are is East Anglia, a place apparently renowned for inbreds, the accents similar to West Country and I was expecting a stereotypical village idiot wearing a dirty while overall, wellies and sucking a large bit of straw out of the corner of his mouth with drool dripping down. There's probably a few places where everyone has two heads and webbed feet, too. Probably.

After having a generally good time socializing, it was back to South London and mums's, enduring a nightmare four and a half hour journey. More packing and moving. A few days later after that I decided to visit yet another friend by way of Brighton, in Sussex. The friend in question was a tall skinhead called Reg whom I'd met a few months back at a Bad Manners gig at the Concorde 2 venue.

   Now this Reg is a right character and a brilliant laugh. I met him at a local pub near the main railway station for a couple of jars and then back to his place where he then decided on the spur of the moment to spend a few days in London with me! One of the highlights during his stay was to have an impromptu drunken argument with a defective door on a train separating two carriages and us almost getting into a fight with some wank trendies at Herne Hill station who one bimbo slut had walked up to him and blurted out "are you a racist" while her equally wank trendy mates had said something amongst themselves about "he's black so what's he doing with *him*" etc.

   I couldn't believe the front she had and it's true of the old saying that no matter where you go anywhere in life you're always going to bump into some arsehole that's going to piss you off and I was so wound up with these moronic cretins that this was one of the rare occasions I was ready for a confrontation.

   "So I'm a black skinhead, so have you bunch of wankers got a fucking problem with that, or wot?"

   After they went away it took me some time for me to calm down as I was breathing very hard and wheezing a little.
   A couple of weeks later I was out of London for good and setting up shop in the farthest wilderness reaches of West Cornwall.

   *   *   *   *   *   *   *

DUCHY HELL: YEAR ONE

FEBRUARY

"I have no interest in pleasing the general public at all. I think they're largely scum that you see out on the fucking street and I don't want to please cunts like them." Sid Vicious

Life with Gill was working out better than I expected; in all we were beginning to be a couple again in all but name. We'd alternate between cooking meals for each other; she'd wash my clothes and I'd tidy up her flat while she went to work. She'd make a point of not boozing with me which was the point of all our previous troubles in the past.

St. Just, where she lived is situated near the edge of South West Britain and is such a small town you can literally walk from one end of town to another in the space of 15 minutes; it is also noted that St Just has a reputation as one of the most redneck towns anywhere in Cornwall, but funnily enough I didn't get the sort of reception I was expecting. Sure, I'd get a few odd looks from people but then again I get odd looks from people all the time anyway so it didn't make much difference; however, I was very irritated by her downstairs neighbour who couldn't have been more bent if he had "queer and proud" tattooed on his forehead.

"Where do you come from?" he had asked one day in that horrible feminine voice all gay men seem to have.

Here we go again, I signed. He then waffled on that his parents were Greek, not that I really gave a shit, and left him to it when I went upstairs to Gill's flat. Definitely one to avoid, I thought, especially upon learning from Gill that he's one of those snoopy, gossiping cunts that wants to know everything about a person.

The countryside around here is extremely rugged, peppered with disused tin mines, a reminder of Cornwall's once glorious past. It's so quiet and beautiful here and one afternoon, I was sitting on a hill just outside the town listening to the sounds of nature and not a car in sight.

"I do NOT ever want to go back to London," I was thinking idly. "Ever."

There was a funny time there once when I was at the local GP there waiting to see a doctor when in walks who I thought was Gill's dad who lived a few miles down the coastal road at Sennen Cove ("the most beautiful place in Britain" I once said to myself) so I thought I was seeing double at first.

I had approached him and asked if he recognised me which of course he didn't, but it was more than uncanny that he looked, spoke and dressed EXACTLY like him. She later on stated that it was her Uncle Frank that I had tried to speak to but she really had nothing to do with him or her other distant relatives that live here.

Within the first week and a half, the first cracks started to appear between me and Gill.

I had been in Gill's bedroom one evening sorting out some of my personal stuff when she flew past the doorway literally spitting blood and an almighty verbal ruck occurred. She wasn't drunk this time but I had left my mobile in her lounge and she had picked it up and read my texts.

Now, I don't know what business it was of hers to read my personal messages, but as far as I'm concerned, that was an invasion of privacy. Her main anger was directed at me being close friends with an ex-student friend of mine known as Pagan Zoe with whom I'd recently exchanged some texts, but to Mad Gill's eyes she was Public Enemy Number One.

"Right, so you two are laughing behind my back now?"
"You had no right to read my mobile!"
"How long will it be before you get your own place? Because I want you out as soon as possible."
"Fine, if that's the way you want it, since you hate me so much!"

All night I felt uncomfortable and uneasy sleeping next to her in her bed with all sorts of things racing through my head. The following morning we were still having a pop at each other when suddenly the whole argument just evaporated as if the subject in question had never existed.

The silly bitch tried the same trick of reading my personal messages again a few days later, but this time I was ready for her by setting up a trap to see if she really was dumb enough and stupid enough to use my mobile again without my permission and, sure as hell, she did. The first part of the trap was to leave my mobile on a specific part of her coffee table before taking a quick shower.

When I returned about ten minutes later I had noticed that the phone had been shifted a few millimetres to the left. I glanced at Gill, who had a somewhat embarrassed, sheepish look on her and was trying to hide that fact. Didn't work, though. I smirked gleefully to myself.

"You okay?" I asked.
"Oh fine, fine," she lied.

I had made her look like a complete fool through the 2nd part of the plan, which was actually the first, was to text myself a message on the mobile, and then just leave the phone on the coffee table for Gill to read as I knew she would, as she read the following: "AH. I KNEW YOU'D BE DUMB ENOUGH TO USE MY MOBILE AGAIN SO STOP READING MY P.M.S & SOD OFF!"

One weekend I got invited up to Bournemouth to attend a gig down on its pier by a skinhead from Hampshire. It looked as if I wouldn't have been able to make it due to the usual financial difficulties, but Gosport, being Gosport stepped in to help out. Now Bournemouth is a considerably long way from Penzance and the South West covers a huge area of England. I left at 6.30 am from St Just to Penzance, got another bus to St Erth, a train to Plymouth, a mad taxi dash to the local bus station as I had a tight connection to make which I wouldn't have made if I had decided to do the 15 minute walk through the city centre-and then a five and a half hour coach journey to Bournemouth.

And all for barely a tenner. Result.

I got into Bournemouth about 8 hours after I'd left St Just and wandered around for a bit. It would be sometime before meeting up with Gosport and later on a group who I dubbed the 'Hootenanny Mob'-a unique motley assortment of skins not originally from London, but would all occasionally meet up at the Hootenanny pub in Brixton for the odd ska gig. Newbury, her brother, Sittingbourne Mark-they all made an appearance. But it weren't the surprise I'd hope cos I'd let slip cryptically that I'd be coming to tonight's gig.

The Skabilly Rebels, an outfit of Roddy Radiation, formerly of one-time Two-Tone Band The Specials, and some other musicians, were an unusual combo of ska and rockabilly that was headlining. So of course there'd be a fair amount of rockabillys at the gig. Now rockabillys, it has to be said, and this is for anyone not into alternative music, are a lot different from, and this is important, not to be confused with psychobillies. I've been to gigs before in the past where's there's rockabillys and from my experience it seems a lot of them have this nasty, inept, small town redneck attitude bordering on practically ignorant fascism, so I was going to give them a wide berth as far away from them as I can, especially when I was beginning to feel uncomfortable getting constantly glared at by one of the cunts while I was at the bar getting in a round.

Once again, as usual, I didn't bother to say anything but bit my lip and kept my thoughts to myself.

The rockabillys wouldn't mix with the skinheads and the skinheads certainly didn't want anything to do with the rockabillys, who were more interested in chatting amongst the ordinary casuals.

I also met up with two local skins I hadn't seen in years, Big Ady and Eddie. So I had a top night getting slaughtered, lots of piss taking and getting to know various people, including a well fit, and very well endowed woman called Vody who I danced and eventually copped of with. The woman of my dreams and it finally happened. (We were later to keep in touch briefly via Facebook and several telephone calls but, as usual, in a long, long line of succession of women, she was just another piss taker who revealed she was already married with kids. Why do I always seem to attract these women, ponder romantically about them and end up emotionally hurt again? Will I never learn, hmmm?)

When the gig had ended and everyone had fucked off and gone their separate ways, Gosport had kindly driven a further 50 miles east back to where he lived-Gosport-on the opposite side of Portsmouth Harbour, facing the city. I had nowhere else to stay for the night (I did ask Eddie but he politely turned me down.)
I had passed out during the car journey but had woken up just before we had arrived at his home. The following morning I was treated to a full English brekkie, met his missus and the kids, got dropped off at the Gosport ferry terminal AND was provided with a free ticket, all courtesy of Gosport.

Generosity is certainly a unique thing in some people and I'll never forget Gosport's because one day I'll return that favour back.

I'd never been on the Gosport ferry before so when I did for the first and so far only time, I thoroughly enjoyed it. The Portsmouth skyline, along with the various warships and the dockyard downstream were unique to see. Dammit, I wish I'd taken my camera and been a bit more prepared as this was a great view as you approach Portsmouth Harbour Station from the ferry. Ah, they'll be other times.

   I discovered that the same coach service I'd got from Plymouth to Bournemouth also stopped at Portsmouth on its' massive South Coast route stretching from Penzance in the west to Brighton in the east, a distance of more than 280 miles. So that was handy. Even more remarkable was the fact that I didn't have to pay anything extra either because it was the same bus staff I saw and chatted 24 hours ago on the previous leg of journey and they kindly said I didn't have to pay the difference. What were the odds on a coincidence like that, I wondered. It's good when I have the rare bit of good luck, mind you though it was a mind boggling seven hour nightmare journey that I had to endure at the end of it....

                        *   *   *   *   *

MARCH
"Give it another five or six generations and the human race will cease to exist, what with this world being so fucked up."

   A couple of days into the new month, I finally left Mad Gill's and moved into a large room in what was a former guest house called Endsleigh, owed by Brad, originally from Stoke-On-Trent who had once served in Her Majesty's RN, together with his on-off girlfriend/ex-wife. The house was on the busy St Ives Road in Carbis Bay, 10 miles up the coast from where I had been staying at St Just. The room was quite smart: double bed, chest of drawers, built in wall cupboard and further at the back partitioned of by a tall, double set wooden slatted set of doors was a sofa chair, another set of drawers and a small shower room next door. I'd never rented a room which had its own wash basin and shower room before, so really it was more like a tiny bedsit but without cooking facilities.

   Within three days I was beginning to loathe being here already. As the house is situated right on the main road, it's constantly noisy even though the room was situated at the back of the house; at the night when I'm trying to sleep it's the sounds of doors banging outside my room; the walls and the ceiling are very thin so I always hear people talking quite clearly, practically word for word. I've always hated house sharing because there's always a lot of problems associated with it; and I was dreading that fact that yet again I was forced to, for the fifth time in my miserable life.

   I had recently said to an acquaintance of mine who I'll refer to as Leyton as he's from that part of East London, and he himself being a fellow Palace fan and ska music lover, but too much of a pisshead for my liking, that there doesn't seem to be any direction in my life no matter how hard I try to sort my life out and he quite agreed, seeing that he himself had been the latest victim of the now worldwide recession, having lost his last job in the building industry- and dumped by his girlfriend at the same time.

   A somewhat double blow which was to have unwittingly the same effect on me in a few months' time.

   There were several other people also house sharing here, including an Irishman called Gerry whose favourite daily pastime was drinking copious amounts of white cider, Nick, who spent every spare moment chatting to the whole world on Facebook, the social network site and the devil's bastard invention that has now outstripped Myspace as the world's most popular chat site and is slowly taking over the world (*dun dun durrrrrr! Hell, does anyone actually use Myspace anymore?)*; Vince who was supposedly a technological wizz kid when it came to anything resembling a computer and Pete the Professor, a retired teacher and apparent ex-original '76 punk (or so he claimed.)

It was understood that we all chip in £15 a week for preparation of dinner every day which seemed very fair and the whole structure was based on a commune. It would take another month before the local Penwith Council would pay for the bulk of my housing and council tax benefit because what savings I had was slowly being withdrawn illegally from my building society account by Broomleigh Housing in Bromley (which I subsequently got back) so money, yet again was a bit tight.

I thought I was getting along fairly well with the other occupants. But after three days, they had other ideas it seemed.

I was using the computer in the spare room one evening printing of some literature from a story website when Nick pops his head past and then proceeds to have a pop at me for apparently using the computer too much, to which I turned around and looked at him incredulously before walking out. His real reason for all this unnecessary fuss was that he couldn't bear the thought of anyone else using the computer other than himself as Facebook had consumed him, the poor bastard.
The next day while drinking with Gerry the Pisshead, some dinner was made for me and I think I had promised that I would wash up afterwards. But because I had drunk a fair amount of white cider (one can alone is enough to get me a bit tipsy) I fell asleep in my bedroom having forgotten about any washing to be done whatsoever. But the way they were waffling on about it a few hours later and most of the following morning, you would've thought I'd attempted to steal the Crown Jewels.

The following day I decided to spend the day at nearby St Ives, one and a half miles away which takes around 30 minutes to walk to. It's a charming coastal town which gets too horribly touristy in the summer season and is an absolute nightmare for the locals, but now at this period in Spring, it's just about right. The town centre itself, with its curious bric-a-brac shops dotted around the place was not designed for heavy traffic and all the roads are virtually one-lane so all the local buses approaching and leaving St Ives from the south have to depart from a tiny car park at the approach to the local railway terminus. The station itself, a shadow of its former once glorious past, is nothing more than a glorified long station halt with a bus shelter posing as a waiting room.

The rest of the town centre itself is very beautiful and from a vantage point on St Ives Road on the approach to the town down a steep hill, has spectacular views of the town, the small harbour, the beaches and the Atlantic Coast.

I spent some time in the local library as I hated the thought of returning back to Endsleigh. To tell the truth, I hated the thought of returning back to Endsleigh full stop. But I had to at some point as there was now a sharp chill in the air whereas a few hours before it had been nice and sunny.

I decided to take the popular coastal path route, which forms part of the massive South West Coastal Path, back to Carbis Bay, therefore avoiding having to put up with the constant stream of noisy traffic along the St Ives Road. Most of this route is uphill so it's a very steep climb to walk and you really need to be super fit. Luckily I'm used to walking fairly long distances so it didn't really bother me too much.

When I begrudgingly returned to Endsleigh, I knocked on Gerry's door to give him a bottle of white cider I'd bought for him. He came out, instantaneously complained about me not doing the washing up last night, took the bottle out of my hand roughly and slammed the door shut.

I shrugged and went up to my bedroom for a while. I later came downstairs to join two of the residents for some spaghetti bolognese but I'd lost my appetite even before I reached the dining table and didn't join in any banter as I was feeling uneasy. I deliberately decided not to eat too much so I made an excuse and left to clean my dish and the other utensils floating about in the warm, dirty water in the sink. I finished up and was about to return to my room when Brad and Pete the Professor came into the kitchen to do some clothes washing and it

was only then that they both said something which I found absolutely astounding.
The rest of the residents had apparently all had a house meeting in my absence about why I hadn't washed up last night.

"Christ's sake, isn't all this a bit petty? So I forgot to wash the dishes, bloody hell, anyone would've thought I'd committed mass murder the way everyone's bloody going on about it!"
"Seeing that Gerry had no part to do with the cooking itself," Brad said, "he's going to have a grudge for a while."

I gave up and angrily returned to my bedroom.
I have always avoided confrontation because I don't know how to, or can't seem to argue with people that have pissed me off, a trait all mild mannered people like me seem to have. Especially people that turn into turncoats and one-dimensional bunch of idiots that would actually have to hold a bloody meeting to discuss something so fucking trivial as to the washing not being done.

And we're talking about supposedly mature, middle age men here.

MAY *Care work adventures with Cornwall Care*

A week into the new month, I was settling into a recent job I'd started as a care worker at the nearby Trewartha Nursing Home on the Trewartha housing estate, for elderly people suffering from dementia, just a six minute walk from where I live. Ideal, as it meant not having to spend much time at Endsleigh anymore with a bunch of middle age morons.
Within the space of a few days I discovered that this workplace, just like any other that has a high percentage of female workers than male workers has its large share of gossips and backstabbers but on a far larger and nastier scale. Half the staff were giving me the silent treatment which suited me fine as I work far better and faster alone

without the help of a bunch of arrogant female dumbfucks and this included one that was constantly trying to make me look stupid, called Pat 'Glamorous Granny", who despite her age looked young and fit.

During an evening shift there was an incident where one of the residents had dressed himself up; nothing wrong with that you might think, as a few of the residents here are capable of doing just that; I hadn't noticed that he had tucked his pyjamas underneath his day trousers and Glamorous Granny had spotted this and practically ordered me to redress him even though she had no authority to do so.

A while later one of the residents had slipped and fallen down onto the ground. He was being assisted by some of the staff. I was about to deliver some clean laundry to a resident's bedroom when she once again sticks her oar in.

"Well go on then, help him," she beckoned at me sarcastically, while at the same time looking on and not doing anything about the situation herself as there were already three other staff helping him up.

Now I'll admit I'm not the brightest flame in the candle in a lot of situations and can be slow to get off the mark most of the time. That's just me. Can't change what I was born with, I'm afraid. But what happened that night left me seething and I wanted to confront her after work but one of the few decent staff who I got on really well had been observing what was going on for some time and had been appalled.

"Let it drop and leave it for now," Heamoor Karen had said to me, in an assuring way to make me feel more comfortable. "But if it happens again, report it to the duty manageress."

The problem with me, and it always will be a problem if I can't seem to control my battered emotions, is that if someone or something has pissed me off, I'll dwell on it and let it fester. I'll then have a severe grudge for ages. Gotta finally learn to be assertive and firm with people, probably would feel a lot more happier about myself then.

"That bloody Pat made me look a cunt. And that's something I'm not about to forget in a hurry."

A care assistant's job has always been a pretty grim, badly paid, stressful job. Working with dementia residents is even more demanding and stressful when you consider that there are various and extreme forms of dementia which affects different people in different ways. This in turn causes most residents to have severe mood swings which will often lead to violence. I've been spat at, punched, scratched, verbally abused and you just have to sit there and take it. Many times have I heard the usual "I dunno how you can do a job like that" to which I would reply "well, that's an irrespective statement seeing how I couldn't do a policeman's or prison officer's job."

There were two female care assistants who I loathed that could gossip their way for England at the Olympic Games. They both had a harsh and horrible Lancashire accent, and they reminded me of the classic Les Dawson and Roy Barraclough characters Cissy and Ada and luckily I didn't get assigned to work with them too often but when I did on the odd occasion, it was horrendous.
One of them was due to leave soon as she wanted to return to her family up North. Good bleedin' riddance. Her leaving do was coming and Heamoor Karen had asked if I would attend.

"What am I, a hypocrite? She knows I can't stand the sight of her and vice versa and the sooner she pisses off, the better."

However, the leaving do was on a shift I was working so it was unavoidable. I gave her some decorum, swallowed my pride, hugged her and wished her best wishes to the future to which I surprisingly got a peck on the cheek.

Some of the residents are unfortunately incoherent, babble to themselves and walk around aimlessly; I look at some of these wretched people and think that has to be a living hell and hope to hell I never end up like that if I'm ever unlucky enough to reach elderly age. Mind you, it helps if you have the sort of slapstick mentality I have and nothing gives me greater pleasure than to put a smile on a resident's and make 'em laugh which I manage to do with some of them, which was something half the care workers who'd been here for years couldn't do, adding more resentment towards me. The new politically correct term for residents is "service users". I dunno which so-called bright spark came up with a term like that but I for one have and never will use it.

*   *   *   *   *   *   *

(A lull from work...and the curse of Harry Potter)

One day while travelling on a bus into Penzance, I was reading one the books from the *Harry Potter* series by JK Rowling. I was interrupted by a child who exclaimed "Harry Potter!" and pointed at the book. Hmm, I thought and carried on reading.

When the same thing happened a week or so later but was travelling by train to see my mother, I was beginning to think that Harry Potter must be the greatest thing to hit Cornwall and the South West since running water reached this far west of the River Tamar.

A few weeks later while I was travelling on a bus I was sitting next to a woman but on the aisle side of the bus reading another Harry Potter novel. Once again I was interrupted, this time by the woman sitting next to me, waffling on about Harry bloody Potter and JK Rowling as if it was the greatest thing since the concept of God.

I wonder if Enid Blyton ever had this problem with her *Noddy* books?

* * * * * * * *

 Due to a rare stroke of good luck, I was appointed a support worker called Adrienne from an organization called Stonham U based in St Austell but had branches countywide including Penzance. Now support workers are basically social workers but a hell of a lot more supportive. Social workers, and this reputation is well justified I can tell you, based on my experiences with them, are a bunch of useless morons who are very, very good at giving out basic (but usually useless) advice and being extremely patronizing about it, but when it comes down to the nitty gritty, they remarkably do a disappearing act.

 It was Adrienne who sorted out my benefits because they were in an utter and total mess due to the incompetence of the local council (they too, have a reputation, also well justified, to be a bunch of useless morons too) and it was Adrienne who gave me the RIGHT advice on how to get a concessionary bus pass which I eventually got a few weeks later as I was eligible through some legal loophole on the grounds of mental health.

 As opposed to my bloody social worker whom I've just seen once in the last two and a half months who had almost seem reluctant to help with the concessionary pass thing and everything else so in the end, I dismissed him altogether and refused to see him. But because I was still having problems receiving my social benefit, I was once again penniless for the second time in my life and was living off my bank overdraft. All this was about to change thanks to Adrienne but I had to wait two months before I got any money as I still had to work a month and a half in lieu…

JUNE: MAD CORNISH MONSTER PSYCHO BITCH FROM THE 7 DEPTHS OF HELL RESURFACES
"All Cornish women are absolutely barking mad"

My friends had warned me.

Mum had warned me.

For some people, it takes practically a whole lifetime to learn from a mistake.
And for some people, they will keep making that same mistake until common sense finally prevails and sinks in a realise it IS a mistake.

I, was one of these people.

I had never seemed to have learnt from any of my mistakes, especially when it came to people in general. Mad Gill was a mistake from day one and I was too thick headed to realise that. To give you some idea of what Gill was really all about, when I was still living in Exeter and Gill had returned back to Cornwall after splitting up yet again, this time instead of just sending nasty, vicious texts which was her forte, she then sends racially incited texts which was a new low, even for her.
Mind you, I had the last laugh on her that time when I informed the Devon and Cornwall Constabulary on that one and the smile was soon wiped of her ugly mug when the local police came knocking at her door one day out of the blue.
It finally sunk in at last that after all this abasement from her, no matter how many times we'd discussed things-no matter how many times I gave her second chances she always would be the same Gill. A violent, psychotic, drunken, obsessive monster.

Which I found to my cost on the night of Saturday the 13th, thirteen being the ironic number.

Mad Gill had just moved to a small flat, part of a house conversion near the centre of Penzance. Even she had found it too much living in St Just after barely six months even though she has distant relatives (note: Cornish families are BIG. Uncles, aunts, cousins, second cousins, fourth cousins once removed and so on) who live there but never acknowledge her. We had actually discussed the possibility of one day properly sharing her place together because only a few days ago she had decided to give our fragile relationship a go yet again as a couple.

How many times is that now? Three? Or was that four?
Talk about glutton for punishment.

"I'll, er, think about it," I lied.

We got a Fosters 10-pack, demolished that and then decided to go to the Longboat pub, but first stopping off at the 'Humpty' pub for a swift bottled beer each. Actually it was my idea to go out by myself in the first place, but she wanted to tag along. I hesitated, but her mind was set and there was no shifting it. One thing about Gill was that she was more stubborn than a mule. I sighed. I knew this was going to lead to trouble.

Especially on a Saturday night in Penzance.

This was one of these nights where the alcohol didn't seem to be having any effect on me and if it was supposed to be, my brain wasn't registering it.

We went into the Longboat where at first got chatting to some elderly Manc who was waffling on about something to do with "Cornish speech" or wotever. Now, Cornish people are a proud lot and they don't need some Northern emmet coming down here and telling them how they should speak in their own Duchy so naturally Gill was beginning to get more than a little agitated and told him in no uncertain terms to piss off.

Now would be a good time for a quick fag break, I thought.

I came back a few minutes later and the situation wasn't any better, really. The Manc had wandered of a few yards away but kept on looking at us. I had noticed an attractive 30-something tanned busty blonde with her mate sitting at the bar looking at me and I glanced back. I glanced back again a few moments later and she was still looking at me; I couldn't work out her expression and I'm no good understanding all this body language techno-babble malarkey, so I did what comes natural in a situation like this: I raised my bottled beer, smiled politely and said: "Alright?"

Got it spot on again. Always breaks the ice. We got chatting while Gill had temporary gone out for a fag and 30-Something Blonde's mate looked on at us.

"She your girlfriend?" she enquired. The woman's name was Joe. Not Jo as how you would normally spell the female name but Joe with an 'e' at the end, as she pointed out. Well, whatever makes her happy, I guess.

"Yes. But you can rest assure that when she comes back and sees us chatting, she'll go apeshit."

Sure enough when she came back and saw us in conversation she exploded.

I received a slap on the side of my head. Half the pub saw and heard this, including the bouncers who had foreseen that it was going to go off big time with her and moved in closer.

Eyes sharpened. Wary. Ready.

"Calm down Gill. These are married men with kids."

Joe also tried to calm the brewing bad atmospheric situation by offering Gill a pint and gave it to her.

This momentary relapse seemed to have worked, for all of about thirty seconds before Gill lunged at me again after saying something incoherent. Quick as lightning, the bouncers grabbed hold of her and dragged her out. If she was trying to make me look a cunt, it didn't work as it was her that was made to look an even bigger arsehole.

I shrugged and carried on drinking with Blonde Joe and her mate Average Looking Jean (or ALJ for short).

"You don't want to be with a nutter like that, Micky. You're too generous and you can do a LOT better than that. Get rid of it."

"Oh, she's been dumped, alright. Finally took me all this time to realise I could never be friends with a monster like that."

A female bouncer then approached me to say that Mad Gill was waiting outside and wanting to speak to me. I sighed, put my drink down on the bar and went outside.

From just seeing the state of her, there was going to be no reasoning with her tonight, or any other night, ever. She was wobbling all over the gaff, and couldn't remain still. She was bloated and an utter mess. In short, she looked like a female WC Fields with her eyes transfixed on me with a drunken hated slant. Eyes half shut but eyes full of hatred.

"Go home Gill. I can't talk to you when you're like this."

Not the wisest choice of words which was instantly replied by a flurry of attempted punches which none connected as the bouncers once again did their job properly by stepping in sharpish and this time throwing her out onto the pavement. She had succeeded in making herself look an even bigger arsehole than she already was.

I returned inside a few minutes later, a little shaken but otherwise ok. I apologized to the female bouncer who had helped escorted Mad Gill out earlier.

"If she can't hold her drink, she shouldn't drink at all, the stupid cow."

Blonde Joe and ALJ had noticed how ashen faced I looked and I just shrugged sheepishly.

"Good fuckin' riddance. Least she's outta my life for good, thank god."

It was getting on towards twelve midnight and it was firmly decided to go to the nearby Barn Club, half a mile away. How I was still standing, let alone walking after consuming so much booze before was a wonder in itself. They were worried that Mad Gill might've been outside waiting for me to launch another nasty attack, but I wasn't worried in the slightest. It so happened that she had disappeared elsewhere anyway, so I went outside, following the women in front of me.
We then walked hand in hand, a women either side of me for some of the way which must've been a bemusing sight (or a disgusting sight whichever way the locals/tourists are inclined to think) and after relieving ourselves in some bushes, we paid £7 each to get into the club and then carried on drinking. That is to say I paid once for a pint and made sure it lasted for ages before doing some mine-sweeping.
The Barn Club has a reputation of the old nightclub adage that anyone, fit or ugly otherwise can pull anyone. Talk about babe heaven: almost every woman I saw all looked like Page 3 dolly birds, all tall, well built, all legs and all dolled up. You felt as if your tongue was hanging out, there was that much totty-but then we're talking about a typical trendy nightclub where this is all the rage with jealous meathead boyfriends lurking about and posing as if they're bleedin' John Travolta out of Saturday Night Fever and all trying to out chat up some other skirt amidst the roar of the constant drone of abysmal chart music.

Joe had wandered off somewhere and had pulled some bloke. ALJ was sitting next to me in a corner booth not saying much and looking dopey. Actually ALJ wasn't saying anything full stop and looking dopey. It was getting tiresome and tiring trying to prompt her to say anything at all so in the end I left her to it and decided to have a bop to some trance/house music which surprisingly enough I thoroughly enjoyed.

It was now past three in the morning and I had been drinking for about 12 hours straight. I was also getting bored as hell and was beginning to get a throbbing headache. So I said my goodbyes to ALJ who had miraculously pulled some poor unsuspecting lad and Blonde Joe who was slobbering over another fella.

Thinking of the usual 'story of my life' remorse bit (you ARE allowed to feel sorry for yourself once in a while, y'know), I left to set out on the seven and a half miles walk home back to Carbis Bay, not realising that if I had stayed in the club just 15 minutes more the Barn Club offered a one-journey bus service to various towns and villages in an approximate 7 mile radius from Penzance.

It took three hours to reach home and by the time I got into Endsleigh at about 6.30 in the morning-while having to do a couple of field shits along the way-my legs were absolutely killing me, I dragged myself into bed completely shattered and about four hours later woke up with the mother of all hangovers which later turned into chronic fatigue.

Not really a nice ending to a night, is it?

*   *   *   *   *   *   *   *

AVERAGE LOOKING JEAN

There are two types of women that I always seem to constantly attract.

Women that already have a partner and women that are complete nutters.

Jean falls into both categories. There's no such thing as normality anymore in this fucked up world of ours and I've long began to suspect that all women are actual an alien species from some far away distant planet from beyond the stars called Planet Letstakethefuckingpiss that came here to Planet Earth at the dawn of human civilization and somehow morphed themselves into humans because I sure as hell can't figure wimmin out (actually, no man can. Anyone that says so must have the brain capacity of Stephen Hawkins and Albert Einstein rolled into one, or is themselves an alien. Probably.) and I'm approaching 40 in a few weeks' time.

Instead of Blonde Joe being attracted to me as I first thought, I get lumbered with ALJ instead. *(how many times have I been through this scenario now?)*

Now Jean, with half her teeth missing and not much in the brain cell department who can't seem to think for herself, is a nice enough woman and her heart's in the right place but she's obsessive to the point of being dangerously fanatical.

Her falling in love with me despite the fact she has a husband and kids was the last thing I wanted. I suppose I didn't help matters when I had agreed to meet her at a boating lake in Helston one cold day and gave her a reassuring hug while we were chatting and joking.

In the end, her constant bombardment of never seemingly ending texts got so bad I had to often switch my mobile off. Especially after one disturbing text I received about her going to 'fall off a mountain and kill herself.'

Dear oh dear oh dear.

        *   *   *   *   *   *

JULY

"It's true that you never ever truly know a person deep down however much you THINK you know them. And that Karen bitch was the biggest fucking hypocrite going."

There are three Karens at my workplace. One's a duty manageress and the other two are care assistants like myself. Tall Karen can be quite fun to work with when she's in the right frame of mind (she actually once said to me that she thought that 'Jamaican' was an actual language when I was asked some crap about "could I speak Jamaican" so I had to explain in detail that "Jamaican" is not a separate language, but another form of an English dialect called 'patois'.

Unbelievable, eh readers?

Karen G, or Heamoor Karen, on the other hand, seemed to be a bit more clued up on life because not only do we have a good working relationship, but we have a bit of a giggle sometimes, and speak intimately during fag breaks about life, relationships, annoying people in our life…y'know, the usual lot. We'd started working together on a shift about five weeks after I joined Cornwall Care and we seemed to have hit it off instantly.
 I did vow that after being time-wasted too many times by women to really give a toss anymore, the last straw being Vonny and Maxie from Bournemouth (who you will read about later on in this book), being totally headfucked and nightmare memories of Mad Gill, I told her straight that I really did NOT want to go out with anyone let alone fall in love again.

That particular vow soon went out of the window and I can't remember who actually asked who out first on a proper date, but what I do remember saying if she wanted to celebrate my upcoming birthday with me by having a few drinks with me and some acquaintances (which we did, but turned out to be one acquaintance, Nick from Endsleigh who seemed even more lecherous than usual when we went to some hillbilly pub a few minutes' walk away and Karen had been feeling uncomfortable throughout his presence as she felt she was being perved on- something Nick was apparently known for but obviously was kept quiet under the table.)

The feelings towards each other had been getting stronger, there was no denying that, especially when I finally said my thoughts about it one day when she kindly took me in her car to do some local shopping and she had immediately said the same. As I said to her before, I really didn't want to be lumbered into another relationship, but I gradually caved in (I was always weak when it came to things like that) when at last I capitulated and said "well, we've give it a go and see how it works out, eh."

I agreed to move into her house. She didn't like the thought of me still being stuck in that bloody room I was still renting in Endsleigh. We didn't really talk or discuss the whole thing properly which we really should've. I just said yes to her request because anything must've been better than staying at Endsleigh.

Suddenly I was thrust straight into Heamoor's world: she lived in a three bedroom council house on the outskirts of Penzance her two kids from two different relationships, 21 year old Meathead Son, who never did much but stayed in bed until midday and then spent the rest of the day playing computer games and chain smoked; and 13 year old Little 'Un who seemed to have a social disability as he was abnormally disruptive and was forever at odds arguing with Heamoor and both of them used to drive her to despair, as housework, such as simple chores like washing dishes after dinner or general cleaning around the house would never or hardly be done, so for Meathead Son, who for so long was the man of the house and ultra over protective about Heamoor to the point of being totally neurotic, it seemed almost a relief that responsibility had now been finally lifted.

She also kept a large black dog which seemed to have gotten the traits of Meathead when it came to over protecting Heamoor, and a cat. My housecat, Cleo which I had taken from Endsleigh and was my best friend in the whole world got on really well with Heamoor's cat, but refused to go downstairs from the top stairs landing where the bedrooms were on account of the dog.

I asked Meathead Son how he felt about his mum dating me.

Whatever he really felt deep down, and I'm sure it was the obvious, at least he was decent enough to remain tight lipped about it, but all the same he replied with a tactical answer.

"It's whatever makes Mum happy. And she does seem really happy. At least it's taken some of the responsibility of me having to look after my brother and mum. You're the man of the house now so what you say, goes. I may not like some of your decisions but I'll respect them."

Meathead Son was over 6 foot tall and had a temper to match. He also had a reputation as a fighter and fiercely loyal to his family. All the Heamoor clan seemed to always talk about was fighting and violence as if it was some sort of jolly pastime. I used to roll my eyes up, shake my head and let them carry on waffling on about it.

Being a dad, of sorts, for the very first time, and straight in at the deep end, too, was challenging. Here, for the very first time in my life, I had real responsibility and strangely enough it felt good. It was wonderful cooking for the family, to which Little 'Un and Meathead would take turns. I took Meathead to one side once after being fed up during yet another monotonous outburst of aggro and said the following:

"Look, there ain't no such thing as being a hard man. Trust me, there ain't. Only arseholes that think hitting other people is fun think that."

He had also let slip that there were several youths after his blood, all reputedly local hard nuts that he had got on the wrong side of, which would explain why he would never leave the house. All this came to an explosive climax one late night when two of them came down, proper tooled up, with one fat loudmouth chav shouting all and sundry, verbally demonstrating just how 'hard' he was supposed to be, pointing at me and posturing.

"So yer hard, are yer? I'm from Winchester, London. THAT'S hard. You, I'm definitely not afraid of. Hard, are yer?"

First of all, Winchester is in Hampshire, not London, you thick chav prick. Secondly, being afraid and anxious would come naturally to a person like me who has no experience and certainly no interest in fighting. I swallowed. Maybe the slight fear inside me was noticeable.

"Hard to some, not so hard to others," I replied back.
But before the Winchester idiot had a chance to say anything back, Heamoor had squared off to him and was physically pushing him back bit by bit out of the driveway.
"I'm not going to hit you, I'm not going to hit you," he kept on saying. "I don't hit women."
"Well why don't you fuck off and leave my son alone then?" she yelled back.

Meathead had being squaring off noisily with the other youth. I was pig in the middle between them while another of Meathead's friends who had turned up just before it all kicked was standing at the house gate, his earlier bravado miraculously vanishing despite brandishing what appeared to be a covered up monkey wrench.
All this could've ended up particularly nasty if the local Penzance police hadn't turned up after a neighbour had phoned for them. The two 'hard men' soon beat a hasty retreat.

After this nasty episode, I was seriously beginning to doubt my future living with a family where violence seemed so natural to them. My feelings for Heamoor had begun to wane shortly after this, Meathead was getting over paranoid with his over-protection and Little 'Un's disruptive behaviour was beginning to stretch both my and Heamoor's patience to breaking point. I had the distinct feeling that she had become more colder towards me too as this came down to me not stepping in and doing my bit 'properly' when the two youths had come down for a ruck, although it looked to me that Heamoor was more than capable of handling herself.

MARGATE *1969 and the return of the Moonstomp*

Margate, on the Kent coast, has seen better days in its' past. These days it seems to resemble a nuclear fallout. The town was once famous for its pier, long since demolished and its amusement park. When the amusement park was shut down in the 1990's and eventually demolished by the council, it seemed the whole town died with it. Half the shops in the town centre are boarded up and now it's polluted by chavs and immigrants. But it was here that the setting for the first 'Big 40' event was going to be, a celebration of forty years of the skinhead culture and I'd decided to attend.

Heamoor had dropped me of at St Erth station where I got a train to Exeter. It was my birthday week and I had wanted to treat myself so I travelled first class. I got chatting to a conductor and fellow ska and football fan Darren who'd promised we'd meet up one day for a gig and a drink, but like all rash promises made on the spur of the moment, that hadn't materialized.

Upon arriving in Exeter, I met up briefly with Big Martin and his missus Sam before enduring a four hour bus journey to Bournemouth where I met up with yet another acquaintance of mine, Maxie, whom I had recently re-kindled our friendship after unfortunately fallen out.

We were to fall out again, but permanently this time.

Read on.

*   *   *   *   *   *

All seemed well at first when she drove me to her new flat and she had all these pressies for me: a ska ciggie lighter, a cup coaster, a banner saying "Happy 40th Birthday", a big fuck off birthday card and a cake! Met her mum as well and then went for a posh nosh up at Harvester's in nearby Boscombe which included the biggest, most mouth-watering b-b-q spare ribs meal I ever had in my life. Us being us with our mad sense of humour, refused to have any sort of proper table manners wotsoever, we laughed and joked and took photos of each other much to the bewilderment of the trendy wankers sitting around us.

Afterwards, back to her pad and slept on what must've been the most luxurious and comfortable sofa bed I have ever slept on. I hadn't slept properly in months and it was a welcome relief finally getting a decent's night's kip. The next day after a sprightly breakfast, we drove to Margate, which took around six hours because we made the mistake of driving along the main coastal route once we left Portsmouth. Almost all drivers will have 'road rage' every now and again at some point but Maxie took this syndrome to a new art form. She was screaming and swearing at a female driver that drove almost right up to her car's bumper at one point; when the driver turned off into a secondary road she and Maxie were still screaming insults at each other 700 yards away. Others got the same verbal barrage if they ventured too close.

We eventually arrived at our hotel a little weary but relieved, dumped our stuff, freshened up and then headed to the pub where the event was held. Had a bit of trouble trying to find a suitable parking space but once that was outta the way, the fun started.

Or so I thought.

Met some old mates and acquaintances. Made some new friends, as you do at these events. The drinking ebbed and flowed. Listen and danced to some great ska tunes. Took a whole load of photos. Maxie had gone off with another acquaintance called Rumbold somewhere but she had the keys to the hotel room we were staying at. Bloody typical I thought. There was I, pissed up, but cold, waiting and shivering on a bench opposite a war memorial.

   I wasn't best pleased to say the least when they first came back looking sheepishly which is best putting it mildly, and a growing resentment began to fester inside me which steadily got worse. Perhaps I was a tad jealous and I had supressed my feelings about her because she was a stunner and a total knockout. Or maybe it was because every time I've taken a woman out, I'm left like some utter plum while she strikes lucky. Or maybe it was because I don't like being taken for a cunt by a mate. It was a combination of all three, really.
   Either way I knew I couldn't bear to spend another night in the same hotel room with her after she then lied to me next about where she had been earlier and then headed off to bed. We were not an item and there were certainly no romantic issues involved but it would've been a bit decent of her if she had been a bit more up front with certain issues. (Unknowingly, I got some sort of revenge back during the night when I'd snored my bollocks off and she hadn't got any kip.)

   I packed my bags and headed off towards the town centre where I had some grub and then walked to the local station as I wanted to know wot time the first direct train to London was-and then walked back to the event pub where I met up with Photographer Pete and stashed my bags into his camper van.

   Stroody and Malcy the Mouth came down a little later. At least I had some other friends other than skins I could have a banter with. Stroody is a large girl in her mid 20's but she seemed to have put on more weight since I last saw her, but she has the most mouth-watering smile on her bubbly face. I love her to pieces and got a fantastic birthday snog of her. Mmmmm! Verrrrry nice.
   Malcy, being Malcy was doing his best to be annoying and irritating as usual and as a result I dropped some fag ash into his pint as a cruel

joke when he left it on a table and turned around. He didn't seem to register there was something in his drink when he drank it anyway, that was the hilarious thing.

The drinking and fun ebbed and flowed for a second successive night. Malcy and Stroody had returned to their hotel and I was getting more and more agitated having to watch Maxie doing her plastic skingirl routine bit with Rumbold. Two London friends that I was with, Cockney Mel and Linda Flowerpower were trying their best to cheer me up and reassuring me while both slagging of Maxie and Rumbold at the same time, but it didn't make much difference in my mood.

At 3am, I was still boozing. This time I was with someone called Shezza from Hertfordshire and Tall Don from the North Midlands who every sentence he finished with when chatting was with the word 'bastard'. Maxie was about to leave the building and she waved goodbye to me to which I responded with a one finger salute.

"You're so outta order you are," she shouted, so I yelled back "*I'm outta order? Just do one, you plastic skingirl!*"

Rumbold rushes in a few moments later doing his hard man act and wanting a confrontation.

"Don't make me get up Rumbold, or you'll get a smack, I tell, yer."

But before a punch was thrown, the bouncers had stepped in quickly and had him escorted out. It wasn't until about 6.30 in the morning when we were still on the booze that we discovered that we were the only ones left in the entire building as it was now chucking out time....at 6.30 in the morning.

We couldn't believe it, it was daylight! We literally staggered outside, dazed as fuck. I hadn't been on a session like that in years and it felt bloody good.

We said our goodbyes at Margate Station, the last word being 'bastard', and looking weary for the worse and totally zombiefied, got on the first train to London. I bumped into Cockney Mel who looked to be in an even worse state than I was and I collapsed into a seat and slept most of the way up to London. I had spent an extra forty pounds getting home to Cornwall which had taken the entire day, but having not standing the sight of Maxie after just one night made it justifiable.

THE AUTUMN GATERINGS

There were days when I was proud to be a stepdad to Heamoor's youngest son, Little 'Un. He had taken to me in a big way and even though he was 13 at the time, he'd kiss me on the cheek before saying goodnight and off to bed every night. We'd do things every proud dad and son would do together: I'd patiently help him with his homework and also continued to do some cooking for the family. There was however, a social problem that was predictable but unavoidable which I had forseen the moment I had agreed to move into Heamoor's. I never cared much for people's views on anything concerning myself, but I was more concerned for how people were going to judge Heamoor and in particularly Little 'Un. One day, he had walked home from school and he looked anguished and sad.

"What's up mate? Everything ok?" I enquired.
"It's the other kids," he began. "They've seen you with Mum and they've taken the piss. So I said he's black, so what, leave him alone, he's still my dad."

I looked at him and gave a weak smile. I couldn't say anything. I bent down and hugged him tightly. This…a 13 year old kid, defending someone who had just come into his life and spoke of me as a proper dad, and not just as a stepdad. I could've burst into tears right then and now. I felt so proud. Like the crowning achievement of a lifetime's work.

When Heamoor was at work on a late shift and Little 'Un wasn't at school and I wasn't due in for work, I'd take him out every now and again. One evening, we went to a local pub to see a school friend of his to play some pool, which was his favourite sport.

"Two beers please!" he quipped at the landlord.

"Oi!" I blurted out. I corrected him. "Sorry about that-make that a bottle of Becks and two cokes with ice for the kids, thanks." Cheeky little tyke!

One weekend with the wind howling all around us, I took him by bus to Lands' End as he'd never been there before. Even he wasn't too impressed with what he saw and after waiting for about 40 minutes shivering our arses off we got an open top tourist bus back to Penzance, went upstairs, and sat at the back puffing a fag.

We also took great delight in taking the piss out of a family of typical tourists that kept turning round in our direction and snapping away with their thousand pounds worth of camera at anything remotely 'landmark.' But the storm clouds were already beginning to gather around me which would leave Little 'Un in pieces, and me cursing Heamoor for years.

BLACK SEPTEMBER, 2009   *Quite possibly, the worse month in living memory*

They say that bad luck comes in threes.

For me they seem to come all at once in a large bundle. Just after the beginning of September I was suddenly sacked from my job without any written or verbal warning. I had been working three hours into a morning shift when suddenly I was hauled into the office by "acting manageress" Haliwell. I had, according to her apparently lied on my CRB check which for some odd reason came into Cornwall Care's possession four and a half months after I had started working for the company.

Witnessed by the receptionist, three minutes later after being in the manager's office, I was escorted of the premises by Haliwell herself, not even being allowed to say goodbye to anyone. A most humiliating and undignified exit for anyone, let alone myself. One minute I was working with the staff and looking after the residents, the next minute it seemed I was shanghaied out of the place so fast my feet almost didn't touch the ground. I thus must hold the record of being sacked by the same company once, reinstated and then sacked again for the same 'offense' I apparently did.

   In the same coincidence, the promise of an offer of a live in care assistant job with Sunshine Agency, a care work company based in a little village called Chasewater, a couple of miles outside Truro seemed to have fallen through, too. No one had gotten back to me no matter how many times I rang up to enquire if the situation was still vacant one month after attending an interview and filling in all the necessary forms.

   The relationship with Heamoor had begun to sour before this and now that I'd be sacked she was even more cold and distant, and she was beginning to turn into a right dour bitch. There was one day she actually felt embarrassed that I had paid for some electricity on her key meter when she had forgotten to take out enough money when she went down to the local Happy Shopper corner shop.

   "Well, wot's it gonna be then? I either give you £20 towards the electricity or the whole household will be in darkness for a couple of days cos there's one thing you can't accuse me of and that is I ain't tight."

   Another time, she blew her stack and stormed into the kitchen just because she didn't like me watching the football on the television. The final straw came as an utter insult in the subject of petrol money as she couldn't visit her parents one night.

"I thought you said you had to watch your money as you haven't got a job anymore," she started indignantly.

"Wot, so now I'm not allowed to have any fun now?" I snapped back, swigging a can of beer.

"I shouldn't have to ask you for petrol money so I can see my parents."

"You WOT? You were managing perfectly well on yer own before I came on the scene."

"Right, so it's like that, is it?"

All this banter wasn't helping us, especially when her overprotective Meathead Son had to stick his bloody Cornish oar in.

I woke up one night and I had a tear or two in my eyes; I momentarily looked at her next to me as she slept quietly and I said to myself that I didn't recognise the person that had fallen in love with me. I certainly didn't love her and maybe I never really did, deep down. Already I had been making plans to return back to Endsleigh but this was given an unfortunate and nasty boost by Heamooor Bitch herself.

Five days after being sacked, the split finally came when I was unceremoniously thrown out of her house at about one in the morning after returning back from being on the piss with an acquaintance called Yorkshire Gobby and her fella. She and I had met a few months earlier at the Longboat and had toyed with the idea of a possible relationship together as we had shared more than a passing interest with each other, but all that fell apart when we had met our perspective partners in indifferent circumstances. Didn't stop us having a good laugh every now and again though. And 'Gobby' was apt in the fact that believe me she had a gob on her like no one's business.

On the night she threw me out I wasn't even allowed to explain myself to her, something she had vehemently said we'd do if there ever was a problem with us. I guess that particular rule only applied to her when it suited her, huh.

"I think you'd better leave and go back to your lady friend." As usual, Meathead Son was next to her.
I looked at her, stunned. "My friend has a boyfriend and kids."

   Heamoor Bitch then repeated what she had just said a moment ago. She couldn't even face me, but looked directly away from me facing a wall.

   "So you're chuckin' me out, then?"
   She didn't answer. She didn't even have the guts to do that. But I already knew the answer anyway.
   "Right. Fuck it."

   I stormed out of the lounge and slammed the gate loudly behind me, with Meathead Son shouting and swearing something about his brother needing sleep. Which he already was. Soppy twat.
   I managed to get some kip at Yorkshire's Gobby's place for the remainder of the night suffering from a horrible headache, and then the next morning got the bulk of my belongings from Heamoor Bitch's house. I wanted to do so when it and Little 'Un weren't in which would've been ideal. But she must've changed shift because her poxy car was still parked outside her house at 11.30 in the morning when Yorkshire Gobby's fella drove me there.

   "Fuck."

   My heart sank. This wasn't going to be easy.
   I tried the front door but it was locked. So I went round to the back garden door and that's never locked. I went upstairs to find Heamoor Bitch and Little 'Un still fast asleep. He had cried during the night and earlier this morning and had not gone to school. I quietly left a note I had written earlier for him next to his pillow. If I could shift things fast enough without as little noise as possible I might just have gotten away with it. After about 10 minutes I had just my suitcase to go, my videos, tv and video recorder and a few other personal belongings. But then

she suddenly woke up. Without saying a word, she stormed out, both staring daggers at each other. It was a horrible, nasty experience, even though it was not more than a few seconds.

I carted my suitcase downstairs where I glanced towards the kitchen where Heamoor, in her pink bed robe was standing next to Meathead, who was also silent. I then quickly got the tv and video, bunged the whole lot into the car and got Gobby's fella to drive of, sharpish. I couldn't wait to get hell out of there quick enough.

The problem now was that I would have to come back at a later time to collect the rest of my stuff without the help of Gobby's fella when she would be there. A couple of days later she texted me to come round on a morning she would be in. When I came round, she had already boxed a pile of my videos and had dumped it outside her house. I went inside and there was Meathead looking expressionless and Little 'Un on the sofa looking forlorn and pale.

"Some things just ain't meant to be, I'm afraid." I quietly said to Little 'Un. "But here's something to remind you of me." I gave him my Ali G book which he begrudgingly took and for a moment looked as if he was going to burst into tears.

"Thanks for the note you left on my bed," he said softly.
"I will never forget you," I said.

I turned to Meathead.

"Why do you think she's treating me like this?" I asked him.
"I guess she couldn't get used to someone else being in her life, I suppose," he shrugged.

I knew he had something to do with the way she had acted, being he was so over protective, but wot could I say? Or do? Too late now, anyway.

Heamoor Bitch popped downstairs. She handed me a large bag which contained my duvet and some other personal belongings. She said just one word.

"Here."

As I walked outside, trying to look dignified and proud in a humiliating situation, I glanced round at her and asked, "Why? Why are you doing this to me?"

"Because you're a liar," she barked out.

"Liar? Well wot was I supposed to have lied about, then?"

"Everything."

"Yes, but wot about, *specifically?*"

Heamoor didn't have the decency to reply to what I asked. Bottom line is, she found me useful for a while, then when she had had her fill, that was me out on my arse as she probably had eyes on the next mug somewhere that would be her fella. As she turned around and shut the door, never to see her and the kids again, I yelled back, "You make me SICK."

As my life was beginning to fall apart around me, I was temporary homeless, but only for a few days. I went back to my old landlady at Endsleigh and I asked for my old room back and she agreed. At least that was one weight of my mind. That evening, I went down to the Badger Inn in Lelant to meet up with one of my old work colleagues, Mark, for a drink and that eased my stress a little, especially after he gave me a copy of the American historical action film 'Troy' with Brad Pitt.

I was bloody glad I was finally getting out of Gobby's place. She is…or was…my best Penzance friend but she has a fiery temperament and doesn't mince her words. In fact, she actually said to me once that because she doesn't mince her words is that sole fact that's landed her in trouble on more of the odd occasion.

We were supposed to have travelled more than 200 miles across the coastal South West to Portsmouth to attend a friend's belated birthday bash that Saturday but once again the best laid plans went tits up and Gobby had made some excuse that she couldn't go, so this was my chance to move my stuff from Gobby's to Carbis Bay that morning. But when I got to Endsleigh the landlady had already popped out but without giving my door keys to one of the other residents.

Dozy mare, I thought while waiting for ages until a resident I didn't recognise finally came and he opened the main front door as I introduced myself. I had been away from Endsleigh for approximately three short weeks and during that time, some of the old residents had left and some new ones had arrived, all from the North. Two were brothers from the Yorkshire region and they were top lads, the other was a Manc called Lee who was an alcoholic for all the wrong reasons.

Since the landlady, or Brad were nowhere about, I dumped my stuff on the upstairs landing, went out to do some shopping and then headed into Penzance again to meet Average Looking Jean who was in town. Quite why she is so obsessive with me I can't figure. But she is and she won't accept it.

One night I made the fatal and dangerous mistake of finally giving in to her obsessiveness and became intimate with her. Which to tell the truth wasn't all that, anyway. Not even a decent snog either. Was more like lying down and getting comfy with a large sack of spuds, if anything. Pff. I wish I could sometimes think things out before blurting out things because next I then said quite innocently and naively "if you left your husband, would you move in with me when I get my new place" and she said immediately said "yes."

It was never going to happen of course, but I couldn't help thinking I was in a right pickle after what I just said to her.

I had got my old room back to rent so that was ok for the moment. Trying to forget about Heamoor Bitch was something else, however. I was desperately trying to block her out of my mind by drinking too much white cider and smoking spliff and it wasn't working. I had, however, made myself ill again from the stress and I suffered a repeat of Chronic Fatigue Syndrome. It got worse when my lovely house cat Cleo died, a day and a half after I moved back into Endsleigh. Being a house-cat she never went out, but she had slipped out temporary to check out her old surroundings and had eaten some grass. Normally when cats eat grass, it cleans out their internal system and they vomit a little. But Cleo had vomited violently, throwing up all over the place. Before I had the chance to take her to the vets she had crawled silently underneath my bed and passed away. It was as if she knew it was her turn to go. I froze in horror the next morning when I discovered her sprawled out and stiff.

My landlord kindly agreed to let me bury Cleo in the garden, but it took me a few hours to urge and compose myself to take the little dear's corpse out of the bedroom. The other housemates were so kind in digging a small grave for her and saying a prayer before she was properly laid to rest.

OCTOBER

"Kindness is the language which the deaf can hear and the blind can see."

Mark Twain (the author of Huckleberry Finn, which is considered quite bloody racist these days)

In my desperate attempt to erase the bitter memories of my most hated woman ever, when I'd found out later that the bitch had turned her kids against me, stopped me seeing her parents and had kept or thrown away any mail I should've received, I had tried to drink myself literally into oblivion by now drinking vodka neat, something I had never done before. Even close acquaintance Pagan Zoe, one of the biggest pissheads going was somewhat gobsmacked when she saw me downing vodka out of a half-litre bottle one morning after staying at her small flat in Exeter once for a few days.

Yorkshire Gobby too, is now also a distant memory. We never spoke or saw each other again after I left her house to return to Carbis Bay. She, too, had tuned out to be a useless, lying hypocrite also, the same as all the other wankers I've had in my life. It always seems to be the so-called 'best friends' that make me use to laugh out loud and put a jovial smile on my face that also seem to be the biggest fucking bunch of two faced bastards around. It was particularly upsetting in this case because there had been a sexual spark between us, so much so that she had cheated on her boyfriend twice (probably more with other geezers I expect) because one night she had popped round to my place, cuddled a bit and received the most mind-blowing blow job in my life. Even when I had once visited her on a separate occasion, her unsuspecting boyfriend had nipped into her kitchen, she suddenly pounced on me where I was sitting on a bean bag, received a fully-fledged snog in full view of her 14 year old daughter ("you didn't see anything, right?" she snapped at her afterwards) and then scuttled back to her sofa a few seconds before her fella came back from the kitchen and carried on boozing as if nothing had happened.

   All this just goes to show that she was cheap and tarty and liked to play the dangerous game, although I was just as much at fault by not refusing her sexual advances. But people like her never need encouraging and people like me are easily led. Playing mind games with me ultimately led to the break-up of the friendship, but that's a woman's prerogative, that, isn't it? That, and getting as much money outta a bloke as possible.

   Things hadn't improved either back at Endsleigh. I still couldn't get much privacy as every time I tried to settle down in bed they'd be someone knocking at the door, not to mention the constant loud slamming of the other residents' doors in the house. I'd try to cook a meal and they'd be someone coming into the kitchen to do their own personal snack which I found annoying. Or it would take hours until the place was quiet that I was able to prepare a meal for myself. (The idea of one person cooking a meal for the rest of us, and everyone chipping in some money for grub went ages ago.)

   We're all pissheads in this house, none more so than yours truly, but the difference between me and Lee the Manc was that he was violent with it, just like Mad Gill was. The last time he kicked off big time was over some mental bint he had taken back to the house called Millie whom he was more than acquainted with even though he was already seeing someone else (or so he claimed) AND was married. Also he was one not to be trusted when foolishly lending money to him as you would never get it back.

However, by a strange turn of events with Lady Luck on my side for once and money suddenly plentiful, a week later I left Endsleigh and Carbis Bay for good to start a new life 60 miles away to the east in a remote village called St Cleer.

PART FOUR:
The Beginning of the Long Road to Hell-Personal Ambition Achieved

At last, after a lifetime of hoping and wishing of a life in the countryside, I've finally done it.
I finally got my own house.
In a cul-de-sac.
In a large but pretty village called St Cleer.
The village has two pubs, The Market Inn, and about two minutes up the road heading towards countryside and Bodmin Moor is The Stag. What with the economic climate hitting most people's wallets, it's astonishing a village this size has two pubs surviving at the same time, but somehow, miraculously, both are, despite the fact hardly anyone goes to either pub before 6pm. The Market Inn seems to open whenever the publican feels like opening it and with all rural pubs that normally cater for tourists in the summer, they charge 'local prices' and 'tourist prices' (obviously, the unsuspecting tourist, particularly an overseas one wouldn't know the difference in prices, but then again I

was once charged an incredible £3.80 for a pint of Guinness even though I'm local, so I gave up pubbing in the village altogether.)

The cul-de-sac is at the far bottom of the village in what is laughingly called an 'estate'. If a pretty cul-de-sac like this is regarded as part of an 'estate', most of the villagers, which included my next-door neighbour have a lot to learn about life in general. But then again my living background has always been in a city or large town. People around here wouldn't know what a real housing estate was if it came up to them and bit them up the arse. If I took them to some of the estates around London, like Kidbrooke, a suburban town in South London which is practically one huge ginormous housing estate, and the estates around the Elephant & Castle, and Deptford, which are truly frightening looking, I don't think they would last five minutes in a *real* housing estate.

There is a phone box near the church in the classic red design style, but like with many Cornish and Devon villages it's just there as some sort of tourist attraction as the phone is unusable; there was a post office within a small convenience store but that section closed down just before I moved to the village and a few months after that the convenience store closed down altogether and converted into a family house. No evidence of the store remains. There is however a genuinely nice farm shop on the edge of the village a stone's throw from The Stag Inn selling local only produce. Very nice but very expensive if you can afford it, which half the villagers cant. And you need to have proper dosh to live a successful and comfortable life in the country.

The village also has a number of cattle grids at the beginning of certain roads and cul-de-sacs on the edge of and around the village. My stepson Little 'Un once explained what they were as such things don't exist in cities. Once upon a time, in an era where the pace of life was much quieter and more pleasant, farmers would often take their livestock through villages on the way to farmers markets. A cow or sheep will apparently not approach a cattle grid due to natural instinct so therefore no individual cow or sheep can wander off and cause havoc. Must've been a wonderful sight though in its' day.

No more pollution. No more graffiti. No more rush hour. No more tubes. No more crammed buses or trains. And no more bloody general public around me to piss me off. Just peace, quiet and good, fresh country air. Sometimes you'll see people on horses riding slowly through the village, and people will often greet you with a polite "hello", or "good morning", something city folk are not used to and it takes time to get used to, or even adapt. Those last two aspects of village life I would really miss.

Good god man, just how wrong I was going to be proven a few months later. The house I chose couldn't have been worse located: at first glance it looked like it was in a beautiful setting, a quiet cul-de-sac with a large tree slap bang in the middle. But the house was located behind a school playing field and you know how noisy school playing fields are. All that was separating the field from my back garden was a large hedge way which was easily accessible by irritating school kids who would climb over the hedge and then onto a pathway which passed my garden, down the side of the house and onto the road as a shortcut to get from the edge of the village where I was to the other side. This was particularly annoying because the pathway was part of my driveway so therefore technically as it was part of my house the little shits were trespassing.
Another large tree was in front of the house, blocking any view from the inside and my driveway led to the back entrance of two other houses. This meant that sometimes if I was out in the back garden, I wouldn't have had any privacy if any neighbour walked past the garden as what fencing I had was not tall enough and was falling to bits.

What I found particularly annoying and a great source of irritance was that every Wednesday or Thursday the front garden would be used as a sort of 'refuse point' as the occupants of the three neighbouring houses immediately to my left would dump their rubbish bags the evening before bin day. I was outside one early morning cleaning the front windows when Mrs Ignorant, three doors down, came out with a large black bag and some cardboard from a garage, walked the few yards to my garden, dumped her stuff and walked off without saying a word.

People used to say to me that Mrs Ignorant, as I called her was just very, very shy and would rarely talk to anyone. I used to argue the point that there is a whole lot of difference between being very shy and being very ignorant, I'd say a polite "good morning" to her, but I gave that up right away on her account.

Also, I have never known a place where so many people are dog owners and worse of all being a next door neighbour to a bloke who turned out to be the biggest two faced self- styled patriarch redneck bastard imaginable.

Although I've chatted to a few local people, most of them whom have settled down here after moving from different parts of the country, most notably Birmingham and the West Midlands (I was beginning to think that Cornwall is some outer suburb of Birmingham, there were so many Brummies down here with that dreadful accent of theirs), I wasn't really too bothered about actually meeting any of the neighbours, or making friends, and certainly not interested of being "accepted" by people (why would I want to have any interest in being "accepted" by two-faced bigots as most of the people here turned out to be).

WESTERN GREYHOUND MINIBUSES RULES THE ROOST

The principal bus operator in the Liskeard and rural East Cornwall area are Western Greyhound. They operate an hourly service from 8 in the morning (an hour earlier during the tourist season) to around 6.30pm in the evening and that's it. After that you either have to get a taxi or walk to your destination which I've done several times and it is remarkable just how quickly you get used to this and adapt. There are no buses to and from St Cleer and the surrounding villages on a Sunday, but there is a very limited Sunday service linking the main towns of Bodmin and Liskeard to Plymouth running every two hours (5 or 6 buses for the day.) The seating is fairly uncomfortable if you're above 5' 6" as there's hardly any leg room or space between your knees and the seat in front of you; and on a lot of these buses the back end of the bus will make a unrecognizable grunting-type sound, rise about half a foot and drops down again whenever it is stationary. Would make your stomach churn if you were under the influence of alcohol.

Although the bus company operates specifically for rural Cornwall, they are not always reliable because if I'm heading into town to catch a connecting bus somewhere else (all Liskeard services stop or terminate in the town centre) and the time table is carefully designed that the waiting times for connecting buses are no more than 10 to 15 minutes, the chances are that I would miss it as usually the bus would be delayed or cancelled. Curiously enough, no one seems to complain or are not really too fussed, suggesting that the locals are well used to this and for any outsiders ('emmets'), it's definitely a severe wake up call.

As for the saying that the countryside is litter free, that's a loada rubbish ('rubbish'-geddit? groan...) as when I have had to sometimes walk from Liskeard Station to my village, a good three and a half miles away, you'll see practically tons of litter discarded on hedges and verges on country lanes, like empty fag packets and beer cans every few yards.

I shake my head in disgust-don't people or society care anymore?

LISKEARDIZED

"Ignorance isn't bliss...it's familiar. And unfortunately, there's comfort in that."
    President Kennedy to Adam Bernard Brasher: *'Adam-Legend Of The Blue Marvel'*, Marvel Comics, January, 2009

I have personally never understood why a lot of people make an issue out of someone's skin colour or where they originally came from. To tell the truth I really couldn't give a toss where someone is originally from, just so long as that particular person isn't an arrogant, ignorant arsehole and it seems the whole world is like that these days. There have been occasional times when the following conversation was spoken.

"Do you think the word 'black' is sensitive, as calling you 'coloured' is old fashioned, what would you like to be known as?"
    To which I would always reply blankly: "Mick."

The next conversation is an excerpt from ITV's *'Spitting Image'*, a popular but savage satirical puppet show which ran for more than 15 series during the mid 80's to the mid 90's and this sums up perfectly the patheticness of people waffling on about race:

"....Northern Ireland. Three white men killed in explosion, no black men involved. And soccer-West Ham United beat Everton by three goals to one. The goals were scored by three white men and a black man and a crowd of black men and white men watched the match. Good evening, this is Sir Alastair Burnett, white as ice cream so no worries there."

While the sketch itself is very funny to watch, depending on what sort of humour you're into, especially if it's 'toilet humour', the message behind the sketch itself is fairly obvious; WHY do people have such a problem about other people if they've never actually met them in the first place and who are they to judge before even speaking to that person? My next door neighbour before we stopped being on talking terms once summed it up perfectly that "there is a different kind of idiot" that live in Liskeard as described in the following:

I found it quite funny that the locals all look at me with curious bewilderment; while I was once pubbing at what must've been one of the most racists and backwards pubs in Britain, let alone Cornwall, an old fashioned inn house, exclusively for locals only pub called The White Horse on the first two occasions, everyone, and I mean everyone stopped their drinking and turned their heads when I walked in and sat down for a drink. The first occasion was with Brad, my ex landlord of Endsleigh. He had kindly driven all the way from Carbis Bay to Liskeard with me and my belongings en route to St Cleer.

Even he was surprised and a little unnerved at the sudden drop in atmosphere-if you could call it that-when he commented that everyone was looking at me so I replied quite whole heartedly that I get stared at everywhere I go anyway, so what the fuck difference did it make?

The second occasion was when I dropped in by myself for a couple of pints of Tribute. This time it seemed even more unsettling because the place went dead quiet when I sat down at a table. It was just like the famous scene out of An American Werewolf in London when the two Yank tourists arrive at 'The Slaughtered Lamb' pub out in the middle of nowhere. People still talk about that scene 30 years after the film was made.

I saw the same people in exactly the same place they were sitting the last time I came with Brad; a group of sour faced burly farmer types and some women playing what looked like draughts. One of the blokes with no intention of lowering his voice was making it quite clear that "no one's Cornish anymore as it's all full of foreigners". Funnily enough, that's exactly how I feel about London, except that the word 'foreigner' when used in the Cornish context applies to <u>anyone</u> that isn't Cornish, so that could be anyone from the rest of the UK: white, black and overseas people.

I smirked and carried on eating some pub grub I'd ordered.

A middle aged bloke wearing what curiously looked like one of them old sou'westers was sitting at the bar opposite to where I was sitting at the table eating and had been constantly staring at me like every other twat in the pub was. But instead of losing my temper and having a verbal pop at him because I was thinking these redneck bastards were not going to get the better of me, I grabbed my pint, raised my glass, smiled at him and said: "Cheers!"

Always breaks the ice. Never once have I failed, and as soon as he had replied back, we were chatting away as if we had known each other our whole lives. (I was later to know him as Old Phil, originally from the Medway area of Kent.)

But after I had left, some words had been exchanged between him and some dumbfuck redneck, which had come as no real surprise, which he revealed and confessed a few months later to me.

"Why were you speaking to him for? This 'ere's a white man's pub, if he wants to drink, he can drink in Plymouth, England."

To which Phil had surprisingly replied back indignantly; "I'll speak and drink with whoever I feel like. If you have a problem with that, that's your lookout."

St Cleer, which is at the bottom edge of Bodmin Moor, and is one of the most bleakest, but strangely enough, beautiful places in Britain, is locally known for the amount of rain that falls here. In fact, the weather is normally so dreadful around here, it is not unusual to have rain constantly for a fortnight. Now that I have my dream house, with a garden at the back and front, the trick now is to keep paying the £550 monthly rent. In London you couldn't even rent a large room for £550 monthly if on the private sector.

Still no luck in getting a job and the council will not pay any benefit for several weeks. It's too miserable to go sightseeing, but yet I'm forced to go out all the time for several reasons. I've walked from Liskeard back to the village several times before as I've missed the last bus, but the first time I did this was in the late evening in pitch darkness and although just for once the rain had eased off for a few hours, it was treacherous and almost suicidal walking on the country lanes towards home as I almost got run over at least half a dozen times as car drivers seem to drive like maniacs on a Grand Prix circuit. Nasty.

BUBBLES THE BOUNCER

During mid-October, I had attended a free Bananarama gig (don't laugh, you bastards), at the revamped Garage venue at Highbury, North London. I'd won a couple of tickets via an online competition but I couldn't get anyone to attend with me. Outside one of the doors was a security woman known as Bubbles, from Lancashire. We hit it off immediately when she commented on my ska badges on my black Harrington jacket.

She was an ex-skingirl with a tough upbringing and with an even tougher exterior and attitude. This was one woman you did not want to mess with unless you had a death wish, and although only 5ft 4 she was built like a brick shithouse, could more than handle herself in any violent situation and could knock most men out without breaking a sweat. But we chatted and had a good old laugh before and after Bananarama's stage performance and this led to us exchanging phone numbers. As with most periods leading up to all my past relationships, the texts and calls I received became more frequent and more erotic.

NOVEMBER: IS IT THE RIGHT FEMALE PARTNER THIS TIME?

"Look, it's not me that has a problem, ok? It's the world that seems to have a problem with me…. they judge me before they even know me." Shrek

I was travelling to London during the first week of November and had to pick up some personal things at Mum's. Bubbles and I had arranged to meet up at Camden on a Sunday…the worst day in the week ever to go anywhere in Camden. We'd been text-flirting for ages and when we met up again, the emotional sparks really flew. She had been standing a few yards to the west of the High Street entrance but I hadn't noticed her at first due to the swarming masses of tourists. When I did spot her after I heard her yell out, I swallowed hard. Maybe I'd been too pissed and it was a night time when I first met her some weeks ago but today she seemed to look completely different.

She was wearing a checked flat cap which almost completely covered her grade 3 snowy blonde hair, ha large orange Ben Sherman, with Levi's complete with black Docs, and a grey Crombie. But she didn't look feminine and indeed she looked more like Winston Churchill complete with double chin.

Jeezus, I thought; but I always believe in life, you can't take things too much for granted and they say opposites attract. And she seemed like a really nice person to be with so I dismissed what negative thoughts I had and we both trundled of to a nearby Thai restaurant she knew, and after we had finished and left, we walked back towards Camden tube.

Then completely out of the blue she suddenly grabs my jacket, flung me into a doorway, grasps my head and gives me one of the most delicious snogs in my life. This happened so suddenly and unexpectedly that when I finally regained my composure and started gasping for air, so to speak, I looked at her blankly with a weak smile while she stared back, smirking.

However, there was something distinctly different about this, in comparison to other women I have been intimate with. The 'instant love' thing didn't happen.

It still hasn't. I should've relied on my hormonal instincts when it came to this as even though I think of her a lot, it wasn't 'real love' or wotever you want to call it, even though I said to her I did. She was the sort of woman I had always wanted to have as a girlfriend most of my life. Well built, busty, very strong. We decided to do a u-turn and headed back the other way towards Camden Lock. She lifted me over her shoulder and she didn't seem to be putting any effort into it even though she's half a foot smaller than me. We walked all around the market area, visiting all the food stalls. We stopped off at a few pubs where I admitted to her (and to myself at last) that I did have a problem with alcoholism, and that I was going to see a councillor.
She claimed that she hadn't touched a drop of alcohol in 18 months before today but hadn't had a problem with it. We walked back to the Lock, but at a more secluded part of the canal where we had our last snogfest for the night but she was feeling that horny she simulated sex by rubbing herself onto me while I was sitting on one of the lock barriers. It was a very strange experience because I'd never had a woman cum on herself while I had been sitting down and hugging!

We walked back to Camden tube and it was a sad moment when she got off at King's Cross and I continued to the Oval from where I got off and continued my journey by bus to Herne Hill.

The next day I returned to Liskeard and on the train journey down, just before the train arrived at Reading, I snapped at a person sitting behind me in the quiet carriage speaking loudly into his mobile telephone ('quiet' carriage my brown arse, that doesn't seem to mean a thing to most people these days.)
The same thing happened again as the train was approaching Plymouth and I literally exploded at some ignorant Cockney twat sitting a few rows at the back who was literally shouting into his

mobile about electronics and telephones, to which he hastily departed his seat to continue his annoying conversation outside the carriage in the space adjoining the next coach. The funny thing about all this was that as I was returning to my seat to continue reading my magazine still seething with anger, a gentleman approached me to congratulate me on what I did!

*   *   *   *   *   *   *

THE STRANGE CASE OF MEGERRY THE BIBLE BASHER
"We know now whose side God is on."
"England, sir?"
"Naturally!" Major Dawlish to Lieutenant Barrington, *"Monte Carlo Or Bust"*, 1969

   Having moved into my new home some weeks ago, it was now a case of trying to sort out some furniture in the cheapest way possible. For two and a half weeks I slept on one of the bedroom floors with my blankets and thin duvet. I was lucky that the weather hadn't turned really cold yet.
   One day, while travelling back from Plymouth to Liskeard on the 592 bus carrying a small microwave I'd bought, two elderly ladies were nattering away and one of them wanted to know how to get to a village called St Ive. (Note: This version of St Ive is pronounced St **EVE**, whereas St Ives in West Cornwall is pronounced St I-ves. Confused? You will be.) The woman in question happened to be a spinster by the rather curious name of Megerry, a true Cornish name even though she herself isn't Cornish, seeing as she has a slight Lancashire twang in her voice when she spoke.

I can't remember who introduced each other first but we quickly got chatting and I explained my situation.
She said she would help me out with some second hand furniture at a reasonable price so I wrote down my address and number. Handy that she knows so many people, but unlucky for me, she being one of those irritatingly annoying god awful bible bashers where every second sentence she uttered quoting her favourite Main Man and it was hard not to say something rude to her within the first minute of her presence ("GOD is with you…everywhere. I turn to God and pray when I am not feeling well. We are all being tested….by GOD.")

Wafflewafflewaffleblahblahbleedin'blahwaffle and so on.

I think if I hear her mention that soddin' word one more time I just might make her step a bit closer to meet him.

HONITON

I hate Honiton. I have always hated Honiton and I will continue to always hate Honiton. Dave the skin once said that any Devon town or village which has the suffix "ton" at the end of its' name is full of racist wankers and I can well believe that. On a par with many rural towns in England, Honiton must count as being in the top three most backward towns in Devon, if not in the entire South West. I decided I had to go there as that was where a Mod acquaintance lived and I wanted a temporary break from bloody Cornwall so after watching beat Exeter beat Southend at The Park I went to visit him and family.
I met Mod and his younger teenage brother, punked up to fuck at the station but another surprise was in store: who should've come up beside me but Ray, who I've not seen in two years. I'd known Ray since my punk days but whereas I've moved on, Ray's still punk as fuck and the last time I knew of his whereabouts, he had been living down

Guildford way, but has since relocated to the posh Devon seaside resort of Seaton.

We all trooped of over to Mod's place, dumped my stuff and then decided to go pubbing.

This was not a particular good idea as this was Saturday night and all the usual meatheads would be out, posturing outside each pub looking menacing and threatening.

We entered one pub but then decided very quickly to leave as the locals stared at us as if we were going to be a target for a lynch mob. Opposite on the other side of the street was another pub so we decided to try our luck in there. There was a small alleyway at the side of the pub which led to a small beer garden and next to that was a traditional shithouse. It was agreed that we'd have a pint each here and then leave. There were four rough looking geezers clocking us that looked decidedly dodgy and we were all beginning to feel uneasy. We drank up and left. If it was going to kick of it would be right now, but luckily nothing happened when we passed them and I glared at one so called hard bloke as I passed and he shifted his gaze at me elsewhere.

We then tried to get a crate of booze from an out of town supermarket but was incredibly refused service because Mod's brother was with us and the checkout bitches thought we were buying the alcohol for him or going to share it with him. We were not impressed and Ray verbally kicked off and quite rightly so, although it didn't do him or any of us any good.

Luckily there was still some booze left at Mod's place so we drove back and continued drinking where we left off. I woke up a few hours later dazed and with the usual hangover, I didn't want to wake up Ray and co who must have the loudest snore I've ever known which even puts me to shame, and walked back to the station, just in time before the train departed for Exeter, for a connection back into Cornwall.

Great catching up with The Mod and co-but the night itself with all them bastard rednecks was really one to forget.

DECEMBER *MORE ADVENTURES WITH BUBBLES THE BOUNCER*

Meanwhile, Bubbles was another lady who had gradually fallen in love with me but I didn't have quite the same attraction for her. Since the Camden meet, she had phoned and texted every day. Sure she was a wonderful woman in her own right and I missed her loads as just friends, but I'm really trying to kid myself here if I'm ever going to really fall in love with her, let alone anyone else. That attraction towards her was just not going to evolve no matter how hard I tried in the upcoming months, it was the same with ALJ who was still being irritatingly persistent.

Whereas ALJ is always on a permanent downer, Bubbles is normally a bundle of laughs. She also doesn't have the bloody annoying habit of slapping my arm all the time like Jean does every time I say something she doesn't agree with (I lost my temper with her once when she did that once too often while I was out drinking with former work colleague Mark at The Badger pub in Lelant one evening.)

But then, Bubbles is obsessive in a way I wouldn't have thought possible: she'll read my comments on Facebook when I'm chatting to various friends (not that it's any of her damn business, mind you) and then queries me about what I was chatting about. She once said that "friends are not meant to snog and that if she (*Stroody*) came onto me she'd cave her face in" just because she happened to put 'xxx' at the end of each comment she wrote.

Almost everyone does this so I dunno just what the hell was her problem; later on she waffled on about Jean taking advantage of me emotionally (at least that statement was partially true) and then she has a pop at me about a conversation me and Chatham Paula had, to which I had to explain myself. The thing is, I don't see why I should have to explain to her or anyone else for that matter who I speak to, and all this aggro was even before we were officially an item. The warning signs about her were quite clearly there in front of me but yet again I failed to heed them.

   She kept on saying she desperately wanted to help me and be near me all the time because she felt the pain and suffering I've been through, but she doesn't seem to realise she's doing far more to hinder and damage the relationship than being any help. One weekend, she popped down from London to visit me, her first venture into Cornwall. I was playing some Elvis on my stereo system when she actually ordered me to turn it off. Not politely, mind, but demanding.

   "Who the hell do you think you are," I started, "telling me what I should do in my own gaff? However, I will turn it down a little, for your benefit."
   She begrudgingly made an apology a moment later, citing her excuse was that her dad was a big rock'n'roll fan and that Elvis was too repetitive. Or words to that effect. Wotever, man.

   The biggest mistake so far since being friends with her was to stupidly turn down a job I had been offered, something I could ill afford to do especially when the country is still in the grip of a recession. The job in question was a temporary Christmas job working for the Royal Mail as an administrator filling in missing postal codes on mail at Plymouth's main sorting office. I had had an assessment a few weeks earlier and had passed at the 2nd attempt. They said they'd get in touch but after the deadline when everyone were due to start and I still hadn't heard from them, I shrugged and dismissed the idea of working from them as maybe they had already filled in the vacancy as I had not received a letter or phone call from them.
   Then on the day I was due to visit Mum and co. up in London, I gets this phone call from the Post Office saying I got the job…but had to start in a few hours. Which I thought was somewhat slightly taking the piss.
   Somewhat.

UP THE JUNCTION

Every month, normally on the first Saturday, there is a pub called The Pavillions, a few minutes' walk from Battersea Park railway station in South London, that holds a trad ska/reggae night with a couple of skinhead DJ's spinning some great tracks. I had attended there the first time a month earlier with Malcy the Mouth, but even though the Pavillions is only about 500 yards away from the station, we had trouble locating it for the first time and I asked directions from some stuck up landlord of another pub opposite the station who deliberately directed us the wrong way in the opposite direction towards Battersea Bridge. When we had retraced our steps back and passed the pub, I thought about going inside to give this wanker a good lecturing but I think Malcy talked me out of it.

This month I'd decided to take Bubbles with me for the next ska night. She was a little apprehensive at first but I gently talked her round and she needn't have worried because most of the old London mob I knew were there plus some of the Pompey contingent consisting of Brad, JJ and Roots. Instantly she was made to feel welcome and as we were one of the first people to arrive at the pub before everyone else turned up, we then had a right laugh rekindling fond childhood memories of the 1970's and early 1980's kiddies shows but one of the funniest subjects we talked about that turned into a total piss take were trendy boneheads where Roots described how they must polish their bald heads with Mr Sheen to keep their bonce nice and shiny and Brad continued with their fave footwear being described as 'narn bread shoes'.

Lisa Flowerpower and Cockney Mel & co shortly turned up and I beckoned with my arm for them to join us. But they were distinctively offish, almost looking down at us as if to say 'what's that lot doing here' which I was miffed with their attitude so I thought, well sod them. And sod everyone else.

After we all burst out laughing loudly for the umpteenth time and I almost choking on my pint, the landlord shouted out at us to keep the noise down.

The fuck's his problem?

There was a momentary silence before we all continued the happy banter regardless of what the prick just said.

Towards the end of the evening, I left the Pompey mob and took Bubbles up to Tufnell Park in North London to attend an anti-fascist gig where the Welsh Oi! band The Oppressed were headlining. There are very few Oi!-punk bands I'm interested in because of the unfortunate racist following some of the bands attract. The Oppressed I have always liked precisely because they make a stance for anti- fascism. This was my first London punk/skinhead gig I had attended for two years and naively I had thought that all, or at least most of the violence I'd experience at London gigs would've disappeared by now, and especially at an anti-fascist gig. Silly me, how badly wrong I was.

It was great meeting up with old punk and skinhead friends I'd not seen in years. We stayed near the back as I didn't want to be caught up in the manic dancing. Unbeknown to me while I was too busy listening to the music and enjoying the atmosphere, a couple of white skinheads a few yards behind us had begun to chuck a couple of empty plastic beer glasses at us. But Bubbles is focused and sharp, and Bubbles notices everything. Eyes at the back of her head, that one. Comes from years of her doing the doors at venues like this. She made an excuse and temporary left me but while I thought she'd gone to the toilet, she had in fact got into a confrontation with the skinheads, who quickly changed their tune when they got the sharp end of her tongue.

The Oppressed then came on stage, but I could sense that the atmosphere had turned and there was an aura of suppressed nastiness in the air. The band put in a good performance as they always do, but the moment they left the stage after their set a group of skinheads that had climbed on stage to dance with the Oppressed then laid into some punk who had been drunk and obnoxious. Cue exit before the whole place became a free for all punch up. There was no doubt Bubbles could well have protected me if I'd been attacked as the mood as we walked down the stairs towards the entrance-exit doors had become violent and some fighting had occurred as we approached the doormen and there seem to be some delay in the people leaving as the area was becoming more and more congested. But I didn't want Bubbles being hit by some nutter either and tough as she might have been, I still cared for her and was naturally concerned. She took it all in her stride as we literally shoved people out of the way, made our way out and finally left.

"How could I have been so blind to the obvious?" I muttered angrily to her afterwards. "An anti-fash gig and it still kicks off. Some things just don't change."

MANCLAND

The next day we travelled up to Manchester on the National Express which took around five hours and booked into a hotel, all paid for by Bubbles. Over the next couple of days we visited her daughter, a bold, brassy lass, who, much like her mother pulls no punches when speaking; we went into town and to this fab indoor market arcade based on three floors, which reminded me of the old Kensington Market when it was in its heyday in West London.

We travelled in this lift and a noise suddenly erupts out of nowhere in the form of a startled cat meowing and then after the lift reaches your desired floor, a voice pops out, saying "May the Force be with you" after the famous quote from the Star Wars films.

Great gimmick!

Bubbles, in my opinion had gone way over the top when it came to declaring her love for me; not satisfied with paying for transport up to Mancland and a hotel room for us, she also lavished out what I would arguable say an awfully large amount of money on Christmas presents on me alone: comics, comic figure statuettes, three old football programmes (Palace, naturally), posh Lynx deodorant and shower gel, Gillette razor, a couple of books, a presentation Budweiser box containing a pint glass and a can of Budweiser itself, and a few other assortments which included a Ben Sherman boxer shorts which I really liked.

I wasn't too sure how to handle all this because I'd never been treated like this by a woman, any woman. I have to admit, it was difficult to take in and comprehend. Perhaps I was being insecure within myself but I was beginning to feel uncomfortable with the adage that a friendship cannot be bought, it is gained. Again, the warning signs were all clear and sundry to be observed: yet again I failed to heed them.

MERRY BLEEDIN' CHRISTMAS

Three weeks later I was up in London again.
My head is fucked.
I cannot seem to think rationally or make a right decision anymore. I didn't realise it at the time but I was suffering from an extreme bout of Chronic Fatigue Syndrome which is a delayed illness normally brought on by stress and you have a feeling of your muscles wasting away so you feel incredibly exhausted and disorientated all the time. After packing most of my stuff, I went for a social drink with some of my neighbours and the following morning I woke up in a slight daze thinking it was Christmas Eve but otherwise none for the worse. I received a phone call from a local residential home called St. Anthony's saying they had tried to get hold of me last night to arrange an interview for today in reply to a care assistant position I had applied

for. The same day that I was going up to London to see Bubbles and Mum for Christmas. I cursed my rotten luck. That was another potential job offer. I politely had to refused and said if he could postpone the interview until sometime next year, which he accepted.

  I left my house and made the short walk in the pissing rain to the bus stop where there was meant to be a local bus turning up in a few minutes. It didn't come.

  In fact, 25 minutes after still waiting in the pissing rain for a non-existent bus I phoned for a taxi. I knew that by the time the taxi would arrive at St Cleer, which would be yet another 15 bloody minutes waiting, and then another 15 minutes getting to the station, I would've missed my train.

  The taxi eventually showed up. Most of the people who had been waiting at the bus stop had drifted of elsewhere and the bus still hadn't turned up which meant it had broken down en route which often happens, or had been cancelled.

  I arrived at Liskeard Station about 10 minutes after my train had left. I was tired, soaked to the skin and thoroughly pissed off. Luckily there would only be a 20 minute wait for the next train to Plymouth where I could get a connecting train to London. Since St Anthony's Residential Home was literally a couple of minutes' walk from the station, I thought it wouldn't be too much of a bad idea to walk there and try my luck to get an interview sorted. Not surprisingly, with me looking a right state, and therefore not giving the right image to the employer, I didn't have any luck.

  I returned to the railway station to clean myself up as best as possible, then got the local two car train into Plymouth. It was packed, and had some trouble getting my luggage on, but just about did it. Had my ticket checked by the guard. No problems so far.

  Boarded the London train at Plymouth and found a vacant seat. The journey was surprisingly stress free with hardly anyone speaking loudly into their mobiles. Had my ticket checked again. Still no problems.

I texted my best Bromley mate Dore, to say I was coming down to meet her. It was only after I received her reply that today WASN'T Christmas Eve, the day I was due to travel, but in fact the 23rd.

I was dumbfounded. How on earth could I have mistaken the 23rd for Christmas Eve? How could ANYONE like me could've thought of something like that?
But I did.
And it had happened.
More importantly, why I was allowed to travel on both trains with a ticket that was dated for tomorrow? I later on pondered that last question and put it down to the train staff being generous as it was nearing Christmas.

On Christmas Eve itself, I went down to Bromley Common to visit a couple of acquaintances I'd not seen in a year, Cockney Nick and his missus Jackie. I was a bit under the weather, having suddenly caught flu symptoms the day before. But they were pleased to see me and I stayed for a couple of hours socialising before travelling the two miles across Bromley to Shortlands, to Dore's where I arrived to find her flat and her entire block were in total darkness as they'd been a power cut. Dore, as ever, was pleased to see me and kept on apologizing for the lack of food I was provided as she was meant to cook me a roast, but obviously couldn't. Her face lit up when I gave her a Christmas card and two presents, one being a silver heart penchant with a neck chain.
Dore was one of two women in my life I had truly loved. This wasn't some passing fad or crush but I had really fallen for her since we'd been introduced to each other by a known acquaintance two years previously at Brockwell Park in Herne Hill, South London, during the annual Lambeth Country Show which I used to attend with my parents when I was a kid back in the 70's and early 80's.
Tall, blonde, late 40's, leggy. Whenever she'd kneeled down or turned her back, she'd unintentionally show her arse crack which was a right fucking turn on.

She knew I loved her to bits, but I didn't see any point mentioning to her that I was sort of seeing Bubbles, a woman that I DIDN'T love. There was also no point in trying to persuade to her that I was the right man for her either as she wanted to be strictly single for the time being. But then she used to contradict herself by saying sometimes that she was dating some Jamaican guy but he was always away a lot. Whatever the real truth was, I wasn't going to dwell on it.
    During my brief Xmas visit at Dore's, the electricity suddenly flickered into life, just in time for East Enders which we had a right giggle watching it; and then I left and went back to Mum's.

    Christmas Day was pretty uneventful as I was still feeling dreadful; by the beginning of Boxing Day, I was feeling a lot better and had arranged to meet Bubbles at Norwood Junction to take her to her first Crystal Palace match, at home vs Ipswich Town.
    A couple of hours before kick off we went into a café to have some brekkie. Bald Mick had spotted me eating while walking past and we greeted each other like long last friends-well, he is one of the main faces down at the Palace and I hadn't seen him in ages.

    "You two are suited for each other," he beamed.

    After he had left, I sat down to continue eating my brekkie with Bubbles who had a bemused look on her. Some up-her-own-arse middle aged walrus of a home fan on the opposite side of the café had kept on staring at me for a good half a minute or so I glanced back at it with a blank expression and carried on eating.

    "Just wot the fuck's her problem?" I said to Bubbles, just loud enough to make sure she heard what I'd said, as did half the café within earshot. "You see all them boring cunts sitting 'ere?" I thumbed in the arrogant woman's direction, making sure she got the full S.P. "Just look at 'em, Bubbles. They have no fun in their lives because they take everything so seriously. We're the ones having fun because we don't give a shit!"

Shortly after I'd said this outburst, it and its' husband got up and left, clearly embarrassed.

"Good bloody riddance," I murmured to Bubbles.
I received a call from another good friend, Ren, to say he was on his way to meet us. Even before the conversation was finished, he'd already entered the café. Cue usual set of hugs and greetings and Bubbles looking on, more bemused.

"You two are made for each other," he commented.

I looked up at the clock on the wall. Damn, I thought. Wasted valuable drinking time by spending too long here and there's only about 40 minutes left before kick off. I paid up and then we all left to meet yet further footie friends at the Albion pub.
Apart from The Cherry Trees, there aren't any decent Palace pubs in the immediate area to tell the truth- The Albion is in fact one of the worse, but that's where the other friends were, so that's where we went. We had a quick pint each as time was now really getting on and then walked quickly to the ground. Once inside, we went straight to the B-Block section of the Lower Holmesdale stand. I wouldn't be seen dead anywhere else except at the very top of the dilapidated Arthur Wait Stand facing the away fans where Palace fans always stand or sing.
Once we got to our allocated seat...seats...well it wasn't really our allocated seats but I didn't give a shit as we bundled and shoved our way to the section of seats I've called "home" for the past 14 years-it was like being greeted by a long lost family with my footie friends around me. And that is what football is sorely missing these days- camaraderie.
It may have been Bubbles first Palace match but she's a football fan through and through from the old generation when the terrace was king. She more than shouted her penny's worth which made some

young fans at the back of us a row behind chuckle a bit (it was Bubble's accent, y'see.)

Palace ended the match winning 2-1 which left Ipswich in the relegation mire.

The year was to end in a unsurprising but remarkable way in terms of health, friendships, relationships and such: Bubbles and I had it off and we were to remain more than just friends but more soulmates with a close bond in terms of most interests, particularly fantasy films and comedy: the more madcap, the better. We are both hardcore football fans but support rival teams totally diverse of each other, but then even there we had a mutual respect for each other as she went to further Palace and Exeter City football matches which she seemed to thoroughly enjoy despite the warning of what to expect in terms of playing quality from both teams.

She is from the old school mob of Man United fans and is quite proud of the fact, however it has to be noted that she is a 'proper' Red and not some jumped up glory hunting shirt wearing twat that likes the team simply because of the team's success on the pitch and has never been to Old Trafford in their life; a person would think Cornwall and most of the West Country would seem to be some distant suburb of Manchester, the amount of people who wear a Man U top.

Sickening.

* * * * * *

PART FIVE: **2010**
DUCHY HELL: YEAR TWO

JANUARY: NO MORE FREEDOM
"Isolation is safter. Virginity is invulnerability." Kenneth Irons, 'Witchblade',Series 2, Episode 3

Bubbles had decided to give up her job and life in London to come to live with me 240 miles away in England's Deep South. More appropriately, she had been recently kicked out of her own place in Ealing in West London due to some dispute with her flatmate and was living temporary with Mum. She was technically homeless but she had plenty of lolly (or so I thought) due to her job.

"I know I live a long way, but why don't you move in with me for a bit until you get yourself sorted out. And anyway, London's a pile of shit these days."

Already I began to regret making that rash comment. For too long I had been contented living quite happily by myself and it was going to take a long time to adjust to living with someone for the first time (as opposed to house sharing with a bunch of numpties in the past.) I warned her about the attitude of most people in Cornwall and she seemed ok about it. What she was not prepared however was the level of ignorance I've come across.

We got a van hired and drove to her former home in Ealing in the morning to pick up all her belongings which included an African Grey parrot, several grass snakes and tortoises. And a huge amount of books. It took another five hours to arrive at St Cleer and after I had paid the driver (Bubbles didn't contributed), we left her belongings downstairs to get some rest, too late and too tired to clean up and sort her things out tonight.

*   *   *   *   *   *

   After Bubbles had settled in to life in St Cleer and therefore taking over my life forever, which is still hard to adjust to after all this time as I try to enjoy what little independence and space I have left…which is very little these days…she still had a lot to learn about life and people in Cornwall. A local example of this was a villager called Garry, a lad originally from Blackburn in Lancashire, an old mill town that has one of the most concentrated Asian populations in Britain. He once showed me a White Power insignia in his wallet while I was once drinking at The Market Inn. I looked at it, looked at him and then carried on drinking without commenting. If he was supposed to faze me he was off to a bad start.
   He tried his next trick to get me to react was on the night of one of Robbie's infamous house parties which I and Bubbles had attended. While the beer ebbed and flowed, he made a reference to me having a "spear and shield."
   A young female in the background shouted out "only you could get away with what you said, Garry." Robbie Next Door Neighbour shuffled somewhat uncomfortably and then did a disappearing act into his lounge while Bubbles looked as if she was about to punch him into the middle of next week.
   That was the last time I had anything to do with Robbie Next Door Neighbour even though I hadn't done anything to actually upset him, or most people in the village. The so called friends of his that I would use to have a chat and sometimes the odd laugh with had suddenly stopped speaking to me and gave me the silent treatment. Pretty pathetic when you come to think of it. 'Lead sheep attitude' I called it; he really thought he was the cock o' the north thinking he was some sort of patriarch-what he says, goes, and people here can't seem to think for themselves but will believe all the gossiping shit that's being told without first checking all the facts or questioning another side of

the story. Had to find out the hard way to not to be too open and just keep your trap shut.

You live and learn every day.

FEBRUARY: BODMIN

There is a country town in Cornwall I loathe more than any other place in the Duchy put together. That town is Bodmin. Steeped in ancient history and was once the county town of Cornwall, Bodmin is a large remote town three and a half miles from the nearest railway station (the town centre did have two of its own, Bodmin General and Bodmin North, but North Station has long since been demolished and a Sainsbury's built on the site, and General Station is used as a heritage railway centre for tourists.)

I landed a voluntary job at the heritage railway which turned out to be escapism from Bubbles and finally getting at least some time to myself with other people. The self-styled manageress was an ex-Merchant Navy seawoman called Rachel who was hated by many of the staff (and indeed most of the tourists) who scared the living shit out of me after she had suddenly sprang from her office demanding what I wanted when I had wandered onto the platform one day with Bubbles to do a spot of photography not knowing the station was closed to the general public. After I enquired, I wanted to work for the railway, I did a quick induction with her the following week, got my membership card and then I was left to it.
I started working in the maintenance sheds restoring old carriages, mainly doing painting and occasionally working on the tracks as one of the Permanent Way staff. Some of the staff were great to work with but there was a select group that were clicky as hell and wouldn't mix

with anyone. On the first day, only one acquaintance was kind enough to generally talk with me and that was Nikki, whom once again I'd ignited a spark due to my humourous banter. We went drinking together one night after work and ended up at a kebab takeaway in the High Street. I'd just finished ordering when a mother and her chav daughter walk into the joint.

This time the ignorance in certain people was reversed when the mother walks up and starts to rub my right shoulder.

" 'ere, ain't he dark!"

I don't know who was the more astonished or shocked: me or the daughter. I've suffered some insults in my time but that definitely was a new low.

A few weeks later, Nikki, along with her young daughter had brought for me a kitten, which would be like a step daughter and eventual welcoming partner for Sweep, my jet black cat. Before I had a chance to stroke it, Bubbles took her and immediately decided to christen her "Tilly".

Nikki, her daughter and I all exchanged glances at each other. They saw the clear look of abhorrence on my face, especially after we all saw Bubbles disgustingly make a fuss over her. Nikki's daughter took an instant dislike to her.

I quickly composed myself. "Thanks so much for bringing her round as you promised," I began. "Do you want a cup of tea or coffee before you go?"

Not surprisingly, they made a hurried excuse. "Thanks, but we need to shoot off as it's a long way back from here. Cheers for the offer, though."

They got into their car and drove off. I sighed, turned around, went back into the house and shut the door behind me.

There have also been countless times when I have been waiting for a bus at a stop, sometimes with Bubbles and a couple will blatantly be staring, then whispering about me or us in full view of where I am standing or sitting down. Probably one of the worse examples of this was when I was coming home from work on the local bus and while I was minding my own business reading a book to pass away the boredom, a young woman and two kids got on the bus at a large village called Dobwalls, a couple of miles outside Liskeard.

The woman went to the back of the bus while the kids sat in front, two rows from where I was sitting. The kids then proceeded to look at me, turned round to giggle amongst themselves and turned to look at me again. This annoying action continued for a good five minutes before I finally had the confidence to say something and I snapped: "Didn't your mother ever teach you it was rude to stare at strangers?"

There was a temporary respite when I said this. But it didn't last long as they went back to what they were doing before.

Things went to its zenith when I talked to an elderly receptionist one day at the local GP to make an appointment.

"You speak very good English."
"Well, so do you in fact," I sarcastically snapped back.

I had also wanted to add at the end of the sentence "you soppy ignorant bat", but for some reason thought against it. Bubbles, who was so livid when I told her what had happened, made me do an official complaint to the manager of the practice, who was genuinely shocked that this level of ignorance is still around when I told him and the receptionist was severely reprimanded.

While I've been in the West Country for some time now, with no hope of getting a paid job, no hope of my old independent life back and no hope of the quietness of a country cottage setting I have yearned for all my life, a lot of the people here, mostly posh Londoners with second or retirement homes and a huge amount of Brummies whom there seem to be some in every village and town in Cornwall, who have settled down here for a more relaxed life away from the cities seem to be more pathetically ignorant than some of the Cornish themselves which you would've think is even more remarkable seeing they've all come places that are multi-racial and ethnically diverse.

Some of the worse of these people I've met unfortunately were ex-punks. The estate agent who did the viewing with me before I was handed the keys to my house was an original member of 80's Bristol punk band Disorder. He kept on making references such as "a black face in Cornwall won't last long" to which every time he said something like that I would counter-act with typical toilet humour repertoire because I was determined no bigoted wanker like him was going to get one over me.

GETTING RID OF A.L.J. AT LAST

ALJ in the meanwhile had still been persistent but Bubbles soon put paid to that. Her bombardment of never seemingly end of texts which I would immediately delete as soon as I got them came to an abrupt halt when I said I was now seeing someone else. Spurned, she left a sarky remark to which I replied, "why don't you fuck off and stay with your husband and kids and finally stop bloody pestering me."
And that was the last I ever heard of her.

   * * * * * *

As the months went on, I was getting persistently tired of Bubbles' stay-at-home lifestyle. At this time, she was not even contributing any rent, so I put my foot down firmly on this point by telling her to sort herself out at the job centre. It was soon apparent that she was hiding something that she was not telling me about herself, but she eventually felt confident enough to tell me that she was in debt. It seemed that she was always in debt as she never told me exactly how much she owed people and I was always suspecting there was a lot more to that to what she was saying. According to her version of events, her ex-husband shafted her out of most of her money, along with various turncoat friends she had, left, right and centre and stole or destroyed a lot her personal stuff while she was still with him. But from where I was standing that hurt she suffered with him is being directly channelled towards me in the form of me always having to supplement her financially. It wouldn't have been too bad if I had paid work, but I was still on social benefit.

Also, I was beginning to suffer from what must be the most patronizing behaviour I've ever known from a person. (Mum, is too patronizing for her own good sometimes and can be unbearable. But she's still my mum.) Bubbles took it to a whole new bloody artform.

One afternoon after arriving home from work she had kindly prepared a nice hot bath for me.

"I'll clean your feet for you." Or summin' like that.
"It's ok, I can do 'em myself, thanks," I replied. "I just want to have a nice soak in the bath while reading a book."
"I'll rub your back-"
"Look, it's perfectly ok, I can do all this by myself," I cut in, beginning to get annoyed.

She backed off, looking hurt. "I was only trying to help."
"You can help by not treating me like a bloody invalid then!"

Another time, she actually told me how to use a razor "properly" when I was shaving.
I stared at her, with half my face full of shaving cream.

"For christ's sake, I do KNOW how to shave, I've been doing so since I was 17!"

For my own sanity, I knew I had to get another volunteer job because along with her abhorrent African Grey parrot which I'd wanted to strangle its' scrawny neck since day one as it persistently squawked loudly and being hemmed in and claustrophobic with Bubbles never going out was beginning to do my fucking head in. But on one of the rare occasions she did go out to do some local shopping in town, I was sorting out some bits and pieces in the house. While I was on the phone speaking to a friend, Bubbles burst into the house, her face like thunder as if she had burst a blood vessel.
I quickly finished my phone call.

"I'll give you a call back. Yes. All the best. Bye mate." I put the receiver down.
"Honey, what's the matter?" I got up of the sofa and put a reassuring hand on her arm. "Is everything ok?"

Bubbles had once said that I was the only fella and indeed the only person that could calm her down when she was worked up and angry. Something or someone had made her angry and I wanted to get to the bottom of this. Her temper began to gradually lower a little and after catching her breath, started her tale.

"I'd just walked past the library when I was approached by an elderly couple. The woman only comes up to me and says 'where's your black boy?' I said to her 'pardon? Excuse me?' She then repeats what she had said. 'Where's your black boy?' The husband could see my hand curling into a fist so he quickly hurried her away. That woman would've gone through a plate glass window if her husband hadn't taken her outta my sight when he did."

I swallowed hard. I hugged her tightly. There wasn't anything I could really say about what she had experienced. She's now learning the hard way what most people are like in Cornwall.

RE:SOURCE

In the Spring, I started another voluntary job, working for a company called Re:Source, situated in a business park on the outskirts of Bodmin and a mile's walk uphill from the nearest bus stop. You're probably wondering why I didn't decide to get a job in nearby Liskeard. The answer is that there wasn't anything that I considered suitable at the time and the thought of working in Liskeard sounded uncomprising. Re:Source was a good place to buy decent second hand furniture, particularly for people on a low wage who have moved to the town and surrounding areas, and the staff here, apart from the management, are all volunteers. I had applied to work in admin, but instead found myself as a construction worker preparing various items of furniture from large flat packs. Occasionally I'd be on the tills selling and assisting customers. A Polish family came in once and enquired about tables, chairs and a wardrobe. The husband then took out a ginormous wad of dosh and plonked it on the reception desk. I bit my lip and supressed my inner prejudices about rich Polish and Eastern Europeans and politely took down some details about where they lived and what day and approximate time he wanted the furniture delivered.

I thought it'd be a good idea to improve my CV by attending a manual handling and health & safety set of courses which were being held at Re:Source headquarters in another part of the business park. On the usual uphill mile's walk from the bus stop, just before I get to the out-of-town Asda supermarket, a driver in a large white van and a passenger drives past me and shouts out "black bastard." I turn around and yell back "fuck off." This was the second time an incident like this has happened to me. The driver appeared to slow down but then drove off in a hurry when he saw I was ready for a confrontation when I made a stance.

Both the manual handling and the health and safety courses were three days long each. I had the unfortunate luck of being with a group of chav scum for the first course who would stare, gossip amongst themselves and then stare at me again. Instead of taking things into my own hands, I thought I'd have a word with the tutor. It worked.

I passed the courses and was pleased. Hasn't made much difference to my attempts to get a job however, despite what people say about voluntary work improves your chances of finding paid work. What a load of bollocks. Getting home from Re:Source was becoming more and horrendous because often enough the Liskeard bus would turn up late, or not turn up at all. If it did turn up, it would usually arrive late into Liskeard which meant I'd missed the St Cleer bus and often I did. The three mile walk home was fine, but sometimes I'd be too tired from work so I'd nip into the redneck White Horse pub, despite its reputation, for a pint, or occasionally get a taxi. All the drivers including one of the very few female cab drivers in the entire south west region knew me as I and Bubbles would use them regularly so sometimes we'd get a pound discount.

Sometimes, if I was really lucky I'd get a lift to and from work by a work colleague called Steve who worked in admin and sometimes downstairs in the workshops. Steve and his wife lived locally in the village, and although I got on well with him, I would try and give his wife a wide berth as, sadly, with almost all Brummies who live in Cornwall would be "innocently ignorant" when she waffled on about "heritage" and "where my parents come from"...the usual intolerant, prejudice rubbish. Bubbles wanted to pop round to Steve's place to give her a deserved smack once, but, as always played it down and said the silly cow just wasn't worth it.

AUTUMN: THE MAD LOOE HAG
"Upset is an emotion specific for those who care." Damon, 'The Vampire Diaries', series 2, episode 1

My odd knack of attracting female nutters continued when I was in Liskeard town centre one morning with Bubbles. She had gone off to the local history museum while I went into the Co-Op shop opposite the post office to get some food. A blonde teenager who couldn't have been more than about 18 or 19 approached me and said that her mum fancied me.

"Hmm?" I queried. I turned round, but didn't see anyone out of the ordinary, so I paid for my stuff and went outside. Bubbles hadn't come back yet so I waited outside. The teenager came outside and lit a fag. I came up to her and politely asked if she had a spare one, to which she obliged. It was then that her mum came up.

Jeezus, I thought. This was some wizened old bint who looked far older than she should have. She was short, just over five foot, with short stringy hair, battered clothes and looked like she was the result of taking too much smack.

We got talking anyway.

"That woman I see you with, she your girlfriend?"
"Yes. More of a best friend, really."
"How come you always seem so stressed when you're with her? You're too good for her, you know that?"

I was beginning to get uncomfortable about where this conversation was heading, but deep down I knew she was right.

"I got a thing about black men," she continued, unabated. "I was never too interested in most white men, used to go out with many blacks when I was younger."
There was a pause before I carried on.
"You local?" I enquired. I see you sometimes around here."
"Sort of. I live in Looe, but come up to see my daughter once or twice a week."

I glanced at her daughter, who was as pale as a snowflake, seemed bemused by this but didn't say anything.

"Look," I said at last. "I'm already with a partner, but there's no reason why we can't be just friends."
We exchanged phone numbers.

Just then, Bubbles arrived.
"Uh oh," I thought. She didn't look too pleased at me speaking to this woman and her daughter, but then again Bubbles hated me speaking to any female.
I hastily introduced my new acquaintances to Bubbles who gave out a frown, and then we left.

The next day when I was at work, I looked up the screwed up paper Looe Hag had given me and wondered if it was worth my life phoning her and incur the wrath of Bubbles if she found out. She had seemed a decent enough person, and someone I could turn to for a chat. I could do with some friends around this area, that's for sure.
I phoned her, and made arrangements to meet up in Looe the following day. I met her at the bus stop near Looe Bridge, the bridge that separates East from West Looe and walked up a steep hill to her place, a smart little 2-bedroom affair on a quiet road. Here, I was treated to a meal; and her current life story.
From what I gathered, she had been a battered wife, and escaped London with her daughter and ended up in Looe, while her daughter who has two small children had been given a small house just outside

Liskeard town centre. She boasted about how she was raking it in as one of them phone sex talkers where sad, desperate men phone up these chat lines costing £1.50 a minute to talk dirty to some soppy bint on the other line. Bet they would shit themselves if they saw some of the faces they were talking to, especially Looe Hag. Still, I guess everyone has to make a living I suppose.

While her intentions were definitely clear about how she felt about me, I was definitely clear about how I felt about her, and told her in no uncertain terms too. Her advances were coming on a bit too strong for my liking and this time I was strong enough inside me not to fall from her. She had even wanted to attend Exeter City matches with me so I jokingly told her she'd better be prepared to eventually fall asleep as they were that dull sometimes.
"Oh, I don't mind," she smiled.
"It's not going to happen, this 'us' you might think we are. We're friends, ok, so just get used to it."

The following week I had a spare afternoon but as I was unable to get round to her place in Looe, I went round to her daughter's in Liskeard to drop of a message, but ended up meeting her children and having a cuppa. The phone rang when I was still drinking the tea she had made for me, and it was Looe Hag. But she went berserk when the daughter told her I was in her house. I didn't want any part of this so I made my excuses and left.

She was going to make me regret the day she finally capitulated trying to make me her fella. What was it they say about hell hath no fury like a woman scorned?

One afternoon after I had come home from Re:Source I had discovered that Looe Hag had left a disgusting message on my landline phone and all hell had broken loose when Bubbles had listened to it, accusing me of having an affair. I soon had the last laugh against the bitch when we phoned the local police to complain about her of her harassment. I didn't get any more grief from her after that, but we'd see her occasionally on a bus to and from Liskeard. Luckily, she would never approach me and I'd pretend she wasn't there.

I sure do pick 'em, don't I?

TOUGH TIMES AT ST ANTHONY'S

Later on during the year, I re-applied to work at St Anthony's and I got the job as a care assistant at the second attempt. I wish I hadn't bothered. Really wished I hadn't. It was just a mini version of Cornwall Care in all but name, with all the staff female, most of them a bunch of pathetic back stabbing gossiping bitches. In this field of work where it's female dominated; I was rudely aware of it. The work wasn't any easier than when I worked at St Ives even though none of the residents had dementia, but the majority of my work did involve a lot of cleaning.

I caught three of them laughingly attempting to imitate my accent once.

"If you're going to try and do a Cockney accent, try and do it with a bit of conviction," I said to them.

"We're not laughing at you, we're laughing with you," chirped one of the care assistants.

This was an odd statement to say, seeing as I wasn't in conversation with them in the first place. I decided not to waste my breath on them and carried on doing my work.

All care work jobs, at least the ones where you work in a care or residential home are badly paid and you work long hours split into shifts. I worked out financially that I was actually worse off by working because I still had to claim some benefit in order to supplement my wages. There can't be a system like this in other countries where not working makes you financially better, surely. But this is Cornwall and the South West, and most work is either temporary or seasonal with minimum wage structure. And also I wanted to be out of the house doing some work rather than staying at home all the time which Bubbles did. I was prepared to do shifts, including some Saturdays. Weekend pay is a bit better and Sunday pays more. I was asked to do a Sunday but had to turn it down as I said there was no transport from St Cleer to Liskeard. There was a storm that day and outside resembled a tornado. But I got picked up by the manager in the centre of the village and when I'd done my shift I was dropped off again. But there were many times when I had to walk home from St Anthony's after finishing an evening shift. Despite being tired after work, I couldn't continue paying £7 each time I needed a taxi so I would often walk home.

I also thought that the whole idea of care work is just that: to care and look after the residents. But there was an actual set time as to how long you had to actually attend to them before having to do more cleaning work. The work also involved having to prepare breakfast for the entire amount of residents to which there were 22 of them. This took some time to remember and prepare as each resident had their own breakfast menu; some of them would have breakfast in their own rooms, some would have them at the dining table.

Working here, as far as I was concerned, was just another job and I had no intention of getting too acquainted with the staff I had to work with. One unintentional slip of a word and one of them would go scuttling of to the manager. Once, when I was attending to a woman who was renowned for being haughty and difficult, I stepped backward from the entrance to her bedroom and I turned round slightly, but from the corner of my eye one of the abhorrent carers had been spying on me from a vantage point halfway up a set of stairs leading to first floor of the house. I walked off towards the kitchen pretending I hadn't noticed her. Learned to keep my mouth shut this time. Particularly after speaking with a Brummie worker who I lent a sympathetic ear to when she was telling me about her problems with her boyfriend.

I think I lasted barely a month in this job. I was about to get the sack for using a bucket and mop on the wrong landing and that I was apparently too slow. I didn't give the northern twat of a manager the satisfaction of sacking me so before he tried to, I resigned on the spot and walked out, banging the front door as I did. Fuck him and fuck those bunch of gossiping bitches I had to work with. Although I do like care work, that was the last time I ever wanted to work in a care home. I used to see two of the staff whom I had a particular loathing for on my local bus up to St Cleer sometimes and I'd glare at them while they would ignore me. The same for the ignorant Brummie if I'd go shopping at the local Morrisons sometimes.

NOVEMBER THE DEVON DERBY!

Bubbles was looking forward to her very first Devon Derby. Argyle vs Exeter. Of course, this fixture will never have the same status as clashes such as the North West derby (Man U-Liverpool), the Tyne-Wear derby (Newcastle-Sunderland) or the South Coast derby (Portsmouth-Southampton), but you try telling that to both sets of Devon supporters who regard each other with just as much vile and venom as any other in a local or regional derby. This was the first contested Argyle-Exeter clash for nearly 9 years and the hatred between the both sets of supporters would be as fresh tonight as it's always been. Playing in a minor cup laughingly named The Johnstone's Paint Trophy (the renamed Football Trophy) which applies to clubs in the bottom two leagues plus the Comferance).

"You're going to enjoy this," I said to Bubbles. "No way am I not making you miss this one!"

We went into the away fans bar area in the ground and I started of a chant. I always enjoy starting of a good sing song.

"E, C - E, C, F, - E, C, F, C- O K!"

We had a pint each, enjoying the banter and atmosphere. We went right down to the very front as we could officially sit anywhere you wanted and not what was printed on the match ticket. The atmos was already hostile inside the ground but Exeter scored after barely two minutes of play and it was practically bordering on riotous. It looked like at one point the two sets of fans were about to spill on the pitch to have a proper tear up but the police had just about had it under control. We saw a number of away fans being roughly escorted out of the ground and a smoke bomb had gone off towards the end of the first half with some of the home fans starting to fight amongst themselves.

"I don't believe what I'm seeing here," retorted Bubbles. "I've never seen that before at any match."

Argyle pulled one back six minutes into the second half but Exeter scored the killer goal in the dying seconds, the home fans stunned into silent disbelief and the away fans going berserk with rapturous celebrating.

The mood around the stadium immediately began to get ugly.

"Uh oh," I said.

The police had sorely underestimated the security for this match and there was no partitioning between the home and away fans once the game had ended.

"We better leave before it kicks off," I said to Bubbles. While most of the away fans were still celebrating, we got up and left our seats. We made our way towards the exit only to see pockets of enraged Argyle fans heading our way intent on confronting the Exeter fans, scarfers or not.

"Keep your head down and don't stare," I murmured. "And above all, do not say anything."

We walked down a flight of stairs which led directly onto Central Park and continued to walk in the direction of the city centre, seconds after we heard an almighty roar, and then shouting and screaming. It had gone off, big time. Instead of heading towards the station the direct way, we took a diversion, just to be on the safe side and got there a few minutes before our train was due to leave.

It was all me and Bubbles could do to stop ourselves from bursting out laughing seeing the look on the Cornish Argyle fans heading home.

* * * * * * *

DECEMBER: SNOWBOUND!
"Isn't it pathetic that year after year every winter a bit of snow falls and this dreadful country comes to a   standstill?"

We had never experienced a St Cleer winter, but we certainly became aware of one, alright; because it often rains around here, especially when it would rain on an almost monsoon level, the garden would be usually subjected to flooding but luckily the water level would never rise above door step level. The snow wouldn't be particularly harsh but it would be persistent.

We were snowed in for a week once and no buses were travelling to and from the village. Our first Christmas together…was actually one of my worse. Robbie Redneck had one of his dreadful annual end of year parties which three quarters of the village seemed to have turned up and things didn't quieten down until way past 5 in the morning.

Then and there we vowed never again to stay in St Cleer during Christmas. Yet again from a personally point of view, an utterly fantastic start to the new year.

I was speaking sarcastically, by the way.

* * * * * *

PART SIX
DUCHY HELL: YEAR THREE

2011

They're a superstitious, funny lot, some of the St Cleer folk are. Certainly Robbie Redneck from next door was. Me and Bubbles certainly was aware that there was some sort of unexplained presence in my house when most days it would suddenly get cold for no apparent reason in the lounge or on the stairs and then a few minutes later would be back to normal room temperature. There is a local legend however, of an alleged, panther sized wild cat purported to live on the moors known as 'the Bodmin Moor Beast' (or 'the Bodmin Moor Beastie' as I fondly used to piss takingly referred to it).

Bubbles, a self-confessed Pagan used to say she could see the ghost of an 18th Century local farmer who had died on the site of the house when the area was still farmland and wild fields. Me, ever being the hardcore skeptic who I would not believe in such things unless there was firm evidence that I could see for myself and would argue the point that unless I could see what she thought she could see, I didn't believe her. Besides, modern house as it was, it was always slightly drafty even during the summer because the tiny lounge was of an open-plan design and no amount of draft excluders could keep the cold out.

She talked to Robbie Redneck once about this reputed 'ghost' and the poor bastard literally went as white as a sheet and exclaimed loudly "no, no, I don't want to know!" I was quite amazed by his reaction.

Mrs. Ignorant, three doors down, had a large ginger cat, who would always have a bit of a spat with my own cat, Sweep, over territory. Me and Bubbles would be watching telly in the evening when we'd hear this almighty blood curdling growl which would chill the trousers of anyone. The only way to separate the cats and calm Sweep down was to splash a small bowl of water over them, quickly grab Sweep with the risk of being scratched the fuck out of and take him inside quickly.

Her husband, who I was later to briefly work with next year seemed to always keep himself to himself, but they had a young daughter who must've been the most mentally disturbed 6 year old I've ever heard. All kids are generally loud anyway, but this young girl screamed. She screamed from the moment she stepped outside to play outside their house to the second she went back inside, still screaming. I used to dread hearing her and would often shut the window or turn up my stereo loud just to drown out her noise.

My garden fence had to be replaced because the wood had rotted away in parts and the fencing was now listing. I phoned up Trowbridge, my estate agent who was my landlord's representative and ask for someone to come round to do repairs. A few days later a person in the guise of a six foot, well built, receding white haired, middle aged Cockney Wanker came. The sort of Cockney that makes true Londoners like me cringe and loathe. The sort of Cockney that is pig ignorant, up his fucking arse and has a holiday home somewhere on a Cornish holiday resort.

It didn't matter one iota how good he was at his job, his official job title being "handyman for Trowbridge estate agent". It was his banter that made me want to give him a well-deserved smack. Like a stereotypical Cockney cab driver that waffle on about his politics and foreigners. While he was replacing part of the fence, the barrier between mine and Robbie Redneck's house, he started a conversation which went a little like this.

"So what's it like in Africa then? I guess you're here because jobs and housing are hard over there and you have better opportunities in England."
"I'm not too sure what you're talking about," I replied icily. "But I was born in Dulwich and moved out of London for personal reasons."

I later complained to Trowbridge about him. He was on the phone to me within minutes accusing me of calling him a racist behind his back.

"Listen." I said down the receiver at him, calmly but firmly. "Get your facts straight. I didn't say to Trowbridge that you were a racist. I said to Trowbridge that I didn't want you doing up any repairs to my house anymore because I didn't like you waffling on about heritage and being pig ignorant. And you are very ignorant, by the way."

Unfortunately, when a repair had to be done, Trowbridge didn't have anyone else as a handyman so Cockney Wanker had to come. The second time he came round, to fix a bathroom appliance Bubbles was in. She immediately clocked the tension when Cockney Wanker and I glanced at each other coldly. He said a polite "good afternoon" to her but brushed past me not saying anything. I really could not wait for him to leave the house once he'd done his stuff. He had to come again a few days later to complete what he had started a few days before and this time I made a beeline to the bedroom before he came knocking. I heard him trying to chat amicably to Bubbles outside but I don't think she was too impressed with him.

One afternoon, while I was withdrawing some money from the local Lloyds TSB bank in town, I hadn't notice a teenage chav girl who had silent crept up and stood directly behind me. The moment the money came out the slit in the machine she tried to snatch it, but I was quicker. I grabbed it like grease lightning, held onto it tight and turned round to face her.

"Not quick enough, luv," I sneered at her.

"I'm only borrowing it, I would've given it back," she chirped. "Yeah, right. Go on, piss off."

She scuttled off with her tail between her legs, so to speak. I reported the attempted theft at the nearby police station when a passer-by had come up to me saying she had seen her acting suspiciously all round Liskeard town centre all day. Incredibly, she was picked up inside the same Lloyd's bank she'd tried to rob me not more than thirty minutes earlier and had later on had inexplicably returned back and was sitting next to the front window opposite a private booth.

SPRING   WHEN IN ROME DO AS THE ROMANS DO

Panorama, BBC's current affairs programme recently showed a documentary special focusing on the new influx of Polish and other Eastern European immigrants and emigrants into the UK. It picked up on a particularly vile young Polish woman being briefly interviewed on her views and ideology of coming to live and work in England.

"I had always view of England being this wonderful, green country," she waffled in her broken and heavily accented English. "But when I saw all these blacks and Arab people, I was very shocked."

I immediately switched of the television as I knew if I hadn't that instant, my foot would've gone through the tv screen. I forgot that the UK happily allow scum like that into the country to live, the only country in the world where arrogant foreigners have first preference and politically correctness only applies to people that are British and that you can't say words like 'blackboard' or "black coffee" anymore or you'd be crucified. I had applied twice to work at the nearby farm and egg factory a mile outside the village. Twice I heard nothing from the manager. Imagine my wasn't-too-surprised-expression and contempt that a week and a half later after being turned down indirectly that some poxy Polish had been given the same job I'd applied for twice, but was ignored. That was the third time that had happened when I've enquired or applied for a job.

And before ANYONE gets on their high horses and starts having a pop, it's now a well-known fact that many businesses are now employing cheap, overseas labour as first choice over British workers as it saves them fortunes as 'Eastern Europeans work twice as hard for less'. Where have I heard that one before?

Far as I'm concerned that's a main cause for resent from anyone's view and me and Bubbles used to see one of them around Liskeard strutting around like she was Lord fucking Snooty and being typically arrogant about it. Bubbles told her to shut the fuck up once when she was literally shouting into her mobile and the entire bus load of passengers could hear her stupid conversation.

Doesn't mince words, our Bubbles. Tells it down the line and no messing about. They'd be a small mob of them with them either alighting or getting on at the factory stop and we saw her/it again some days trying to give it large with her attitude while waiting at the main bus stop in town, but a few nasty stares and finger pointing from us put paid to that.

Shortly after this, we never saw her again. I was hoping she got run over and chewed up by a combine harvester. Or got attacked by a swarm of crows like from the Hitchcock film 'The Birds".

No such luck, but there is hope.

* * * * * *

THERE'S SOMETHING DEFINITELY IN THE WATER

Here are three extreme examples of people from ethnic minorities having such bigoted attitudes towards me and Bubbles it beggars belief; this would usually happen if we had to travel by train together and on one particular nightmare journey back into Cornwall from London, an African couple had first sat in front of us at a double table seat while we had been tucking into a McDonald's meal. When Africans stare, they seem zombified. Wild eyed, blank and emotionless. The bitch then only outstretches her right leg but accidently kicks me. I looked up at her expecting an apology but received none. She looked beyond me and had spotted two free seats near the end of the carriage so she whispered something to her husband and both got up and left, all the while staring at us.
We glanced at each other and carried on eating.

"Good bloody riddance," I muttered to her loudly. "Ignorant cow."

Later on I had to go to the toilet which unfortunately meant having to pass the Africans. I got gawped at by them again but this time I retaliated by giving her my most filthiest look at her for a full ten seconds before she finally backed down and diverted her eyes elsewhere.

One Saturday on a trip to see the Grecians playing up at Exeter, we were walking down Sidwell Street on the approach to the city centre when a mixed race couple, a black lady and a white man walked passed us, giving us looks of contempt, as if they were some sort of superior being.

"Did you see the look those wankers gave us?" I cried. I turned round and shouted after them "Fucking ignorant wankers." If that doesn't beat all, I thought.
Ignorance knows no bounds. I have to admit, I don't really like Exeter as a city or most of its' people, either. I'm not surprised there's this

ages old rivalry/hatred between Exeter folk and Plymouth folk. Plymouth see Exeter as full of dumb, redneck heathens that drink too much cider and are out of touch with reality whereas Exeter see Plymouth as one big working class dump full of nutters still living of past glories as a naval city.

SKA NIGHT AT ST. AUSTELL

  We had decided one evening to attend a gig 25 miles away in St Austell (St. Awful to most other people, and a good nickname it is for the town, too) to see a local two tone ska tribute band called The Mighty Offbeats who only ever seem to play in Redruth or St Austell. Tonight, they were playing at St Austell's 'premier' music venue (smirk), The Western Inn, a small pub not really designed for bands and their followers in all honesty, a few centimetres gap separating band from audience. We had been given a lift by an acquaintance and we both knew the lead singer, Lee, a Millwall fan.

  "I fuckin' hate Palace", he muttered. I took his remark as a pinch of salt as me and Lee were fairly well acquainted and I'd seen the band before in Redruth. We both agreed his loathing for Palace was nothing in comparison to the hatred we both had for the filth at SE7. He had a word or some sort of insigniture tattooed on the back of his tongue which looked revolting every time he spoke something.
  As with so many tribute bands, and I've seen my fair few of them over the years, the stuff belted out was great, but it was tiresome hearing the same old stuff all the ska tribute bands seem to churn out. "Night Boat To Cairo", "The Selector", "Message To You Rudy" and the suchlike. Me and Bubbles were dressed sharp for this one, but it attracted the attention of some unsavoury types, one in particular a black six foot meat head who resembled the farm hand character Andy

out of Emmerdale, who would not stop looking at me and I was beginning to get irritated by his attitude.

We were standing near the front, but my back was next to the bar and I didn't want to be caught in the jostling of the dancing crowd. Besides, it was trendy dancing for the trendy meatheads and not dancing for skinheads and rudies.

As expected, Bubbles was shoved about pretty much, but before she started a riot which from the look of her face suggested that she was about to start kicking off, I took her quietly to one side and said: "You see them kids that are dancing wildly? Those are Lee's kids. They're all related."

She calmed down quickly after this, but she was still frowning. Black Meathead was still gawping like some thick Neanderthal but this time whispering to his white meathead friend and glancing back and forth every now again. There's nothing worse than a bunch of wankers gossiping in full view of myself, but as always, I thought diplomatically about the situation; I'd just calmed Bubbles down over the audience's exaggerated dancing which seemed to have been mostly made up of relatives; wouldn't have been wise to square up to the meathead and cause a pub fight, much as I was aggravated, so I decided to have a fag outside in the cool night air.

A few minutes later I came back and squeezed through the dancing crowd and back to Bubbles. Black Meathead brushed past me on the way to the toilet. I shot him a dirty look and he looked bemused about it.

When the band had finished, we couldn't wait to leave the place. St Austell, like most of Cornwall can go fuck itself.

Must be something in the water that makes everyone behave like that.

* * * * * * *

STORM

Robbie Redneck next door had joined the ranks of the many village dog owners and had bought a dog in its later puppy stage, an Alsatian I believe it was, he named Storm. It was already as big as a fully grown adult. Great, I thought. Yet another welcoming addition to the already large number of dogs in the village.

Storm's barking was loud. It was so loud that you could hear it from the bus stop a quarter of a mile away and across the village where the school was. And it was constant. If its constant barking was an irritance now, the following months was going to be unbearable. The dog would often be left on its own accord and every now and again we'd glance at Redneck's back garden from our spare room at the back to see it full of dog mess.

The constant barking, along with his get togethers and parties he held, plus Mrs. Ignorant's seemingly disturbed daughter who screamed all the time was making life here for me and Bubbles almost intolerable.

There was no talking to the bloke so Bubbles one day called in the local council when we had had just about enough and a noise abatement officer came round and had the dog noise-monitored. He checked the noise decibel levels and concluded that we definitely had a case. It was enough for the abatement officer chap to pay Redneck a visit and to hand him over a letter.

He ignored it of course, but there were temporary respites where nothing from Storm was heard for several days and then it would all start again.

"I almost wish someone would throw a bit of poisoned meat over his poxy fence to shut that fucking dog up permanently," I muttered. "You did your best, luv. We'll go to the council and then start again."

THE NICE OUTSIDERS

Of course, not everyone in the village were arseholes, Cornish or outsiders. Indeed, many of them were great to have a natter with. This included our postman, originally from London, like me. But he was transferred somewhere else after a few weeks and now we had a South African fella delivering our mail. During one of our chats, it seemed he had copped it the same way I had abuse but with his English born wife.

But of the nicest people we met, the best, in Bubble's case was a fella who kept a small owl sanctuary just outside the village, half a mile from where we lived. She was allowed to have one of the owls perched on her arm, but it kept on pecking her. It gave up in the end when it saw Bubbles did not react not once, just taking it in her stride as if it was nothing more than being poked by a fly. The owner looked astounded while I just shrugged to myself.

"That's Bubbles for you," I reassured him. "Nothing really hurts her."

There were some disused cages which the owner didn't want. Bubbles wanted one for her African Grey parrot. I paid £25 for one of them and arranged to have the cage delivered. It was a big 'un...five and a half feet tall and in width.

It was in a poor state and rusting. But I cleaned it down, giving it a firm scrubbing, and then painted it. The whole process took about two weeks to complete, but by the end it looked a right treat. No longer recognisable from when I bought it a couple of weeks ago. A new home for Jaz, her insufferable parrot.

SUMMER: DADDY NEWS

Bubbles announced out of the blue one day that she was pregnant.

The news hadn't surprised me as she had appeared to have been suffering from typical morning sickness for ages. I'd hear her being sick in the toilet all the time. That alone was a dead giveaway of someone with a 'bun in the oven'. It also didn't help that she seemed to suffer from what seemed like a permanent cold and migraines for which she was always taking some sort of medication or other. Although it is rare and unusual for a woman to be pregnant at the age of 50 plus, it does happen on a very occasional basis if she is still having her periods regularly and not gone through menopause. But even so, I hadn't expected her to announce the good news at the age of 51. I was momentary stunned but was overjoyed deep inside me.

"I, er, just going to pop out for a bit, luv," I said quietly at last after a long pause. "I shan't be too long."

Bubbles understood perfectly. I kissed her lips gently and left.
I headed to the Market Inn and entered an almost deserted pub where two of the local ignorant rednecks, a Brummie and some white haired two faced hag were playing draughts in a corner of the pub. They were the only two people there.

"Pint of Guinness, please."
"That'll be £3.80," he said as he filled up the glass.
I looked up at the landlord. "No, I want a pint of Guinness, not the entire brewery!"
"That's still £3.80, please." I muttered a curse under my breath and paid him. Bastard was obviously charging me 'tourist rate' price even though he knows I'm a local. I drank up quickly, glanced at the two locals and then left. I never returned to that pub ever again after that.

I arrived home about half an hour after I had left and gave Bubbles a warm hug. The thought of me being a dad. My own kid. My own family. Something I could be proud of. I told a lot of people the good news and they were dead chuffed for us. Especially Mum who gave us lot of soft toys and assortments. However, as the weeks gradually turned into months and Bubbles didn't appear to be any bigger than when she first announced she was pregnant, I was beginning to have my suspicions. My friends had their suspicions too, but had decided not to voice their opinions. At least, not in front of Bubbles when I was with them.

Although she claimed she was seeing a midwife, there was no evidence that she was going to any antenatal classes and she always seemed reluctant to answer any question I said in reference to buying baby clothes and a cot. And although she was a light smoker like I was, she had no hesitation of not giving up during her supposed pregnancy.

Worse of all, there was no indication that she had ever taken a pregnancy test with a testing kit as I never saw her with one.

There wasn't really much I could do so instead of these thoughts lingering in my mind and festering, I would take her out occasionally to a tourist attraction of some kind. She never had any initiative to go out to anywhere like that by herself, much as she likes museums like I do. So I would plan these trips and then we'd go out. Planning was essential because we had no car and I can't drive. So we'd have to rely on public transport. Which was just as dreadful in the summer as it was in the winter months. It could take up to around 2 and a half hours by bus depending where we wanted to go so spending time somewhere could be limited as the last bus from Liskeard back to our village was 6.30pm.

There were some great trips and there were some bad trips, all part and parcel of travelling and going to somewhere new. The visit to Lanhydrock House, owned by the National Trust was definitely a bad day out. At more than £15 each for a ticket, this was not going to be an affordable experience and I voiced my opinion loudly.

"How come it's so expensive? It's ok for rich overseas tourists who don't know any better but what about for us locals?"

I received a look of contempt from some snooty nose cow of a cash assistant while I was getting the tickets, to which I icily stared straight back at her. From the exit gates to the stately home itself was a fair trek so we were allowed to travel in these buggy things the house provided. We went in but it seemed the entire house and most of the gardens outside was teaming with about 20 coachloads of German tourists who had turned up (Germans are apparently very interested in English stately homes, particularly after the period show 'Downton Abbey' became a worldwide phenomenon.)

It was too claustrophobic to view the exhibits properly and I was becoming annoyed bumping into someone every few seconds so I went out of the house and sat down on a bench in the gardens reading and patiently waited for Bubbles. One of the better trips was the visits to Boscastle and Tintagel, in the north of Cornwall.
Boscastle has a famous witchcraft museum whereas Tintagel, a few miles to the south is famous for the place that is reputedly the birthplace and home of the legendary King Arthur.

It was also the choice time to visit the local car boot fairs where we would go most weeks to pick up a bargain or three. We'd end up with bags all full of memorabilia (this included a somewhat suspect signed framed picture of legendary Bad Manners frontman Buster Bloodvessel, but the man's my music hero so I had to get it.

We spent Christmas and New Year Day at Mum's, in London. No way were we going to suffer at the village like last year. However, 2012 was going to be the final turning point in my life.

PART SEVEN
DUCHY HELL: YEAR FOUR

2012: FEBRUARY

"Trustworthiness is a highly esteemed commodity. When one has it, one is considered valuble. When one has lost it, one may be considered worthless." L. Ron Hubbard

About seven or eight months into Bubbles' supposed 'pregnancy', and she was still not much bigger than when she announced she was, the penny dropped in the form of an almighty bombshell.

"I...I had a miscarriage. Two, in fact."
I was stunned. "When?" I asked.
"November, thereabouts. It was a missed miscarriage. I didn't know anything about it. And then I miscarried again earlier this year. I'm...I'm so sorry."

I exploded. "You had a second miscarriage two months ago and it's only now you're telling me? What's WRONG with you?"

She went on to explain some gobbidygook about why both pregnancies went wrong but in my mind as far as I'm concerned she lied about being pregnant in the first place. In fact, her life with me after two years was one big lie.

"All you ever do is sit on your fat arse watching downloaded DVD's which you did off my computer all day," I raged, "Or knit all day, you've only ever done four days voluntary work in the 2 years you've been here, you're constantly skint which means I have to pay your share of the rent and bills and NOW you tell me that you're NOT pregnant two months after you apparently had your miscarriage? You're a waste of space, you know that?"

We went at each other's' throats for some time but when the heated argument finally ended, I knew things were never going to be the same between us, and I needed out of this nonoptimum, but quickly. But patience is a virtue, and all good things comes to those who wait, as the saying goes.

* * * * * * *

For some time now we had frequented a local café at Liskeard's cattle market, to have some good quality grub and have banter with the staff at least once a week. Previously, me and Bubbles had never seen a cattle market in full view before on its cattle market day, every Tuesday fortnight, where farmers from around the local vicinity and beyond would come to sell and trade their livestock. This practice has been going in the town continuously since the 13th Century.

I asked by chance if there was a job going at the café. There wasn't at present, but I was told to leave my details and that they'd get back to me if one cropped up. A few weeks later while me and Bubbles were in the café tucking into some grub as usual, the offer of a job had come up and that if I could start doing some part time work next week on a trial period.

The following week on Monday, I got in for 9 am, shown what to do and was left to it. While I was clearing away a table, a middle aged lady asked if I was Lenny Henry.

I quizzically looked at her and two things rapidly came into my mind before I decided to speak.

a) "Yes, I AM Lenny Henry. I got sacked by the BBC and then with the company who do those crap Premier Inn hotel ads. I gotta make ends meet, so I'm doing this café job."
b) "No. I am in fact the prime minister of Botswana and this is my day off."

In the end I just politely said, "no" and carried on clearing and wiping the tables.

At bang on 12pm which was the end of my working day, I finished, but was astounded when I received just a measly £15 for my trouble, was thanked begrudgingly for my work and was told to ring in next week to see if any further work from them was available. I knew deep down there wasn't much point even thinking about it so I didn't bother.

Talk about being exploited. The morning job, which worked out at just a fiver per hour may have been cash in hand but it was a clear sign of a family business taking the all out fucking piss, particularly when Bubbles had answered a phone call from them one day the following week saying I wasn't to come back as they had given the proprietor's son the job to, and made it full time.

I grimaced and then shrugged, as if I had expected the bad news the minute I left their establishment. What would've been the point of being angry? I had wanted to pop down and give them a piece of my mind as I'd
been taken the piss out of, but good. But in the end we both decided it wasn't worth the effort wasting our time. Another lesson of life well learned.

*   *   *   *   *   *

MARCH DUMB REDNECKS HAVE MARCH GUY FAWKES NIGHT SHOCK

One night when me and Bubbles were trying to get some sleep and both our cats had settled down in the lounge contentedly, we were suddenly woken up by almighty loud bangs up in the sky. Redneck next door was having, once again one of his infernal get-togethers but this time it was midweek. Someone was deliberately setting of fireworks right outside our house.

Apparently, it was Mrs Ignorant's husband who was letting of the fireworks. I think they were trying to get a reaction out of us, but we stood firm and held on. The fireworks continued for approximately another five or six minutes which only succeeded in a neighbour across the cul-de-sac screaming from a top window to stop what they were doing. Tilly had climbed under our duvet and was shivering while Sweep had hidden somewhere and both cats took some time to recover.

*　　*　　*　　*　　*　　*

I love my gardening, and I'd often buy plants and do up the garden, making it look spruce and tidy. I would buy hanging baskets for the front, adding a bit of glamour. Some village low life scum stole some of the flowers from outside one of the baskets one night.

"Look at this," I said to Bubbles. "Whoever did this knew what they were doing. The stems were cut, not pulled. If I find the bastard who did this, I'll wring his or her fucking neck."

MAY

Every year at the end of May is the traditional Holy Well dressing in the village. The well stands on the site of a former 13th century chapel which was destroyed during the English Civil War. Next to the well stands an ancient cross dating from approximately the 9th century but around both the well and cross now stands modern housing which gives a distinctly horrible and false view of the immediate area. I feel it's important to carry on local regional traditions up without successive governments of ours doing their best to continually destroy heritage in the name of political correctness and their warped version of 'progress and modernization'.

I'd missed this ceremony twice in successive years. This was the last chance to see this while I'm here and I was all set to leave the house but Bubbles kept on dilly-dallying and as the minutes ticked away, I began to get more and more frustrated with her.

"For christ's sake, will you PLEASE get a move on because if we don't leave now, we're going to miss what's left of the ceremony."

And sure enough, fifteen minutes later when we arrived at the well, there was just a string of linked triangle shaped flags flapping about, a couple or so locals chatting amongst themselves and the priest and a young lad next to a set of house flowers that were being sold to the public. The well itself looked very nice with the flower arrangement around it.

Furiously, I turned to Bubbles.

"We've missed the ceremony. We've missed the ceremony and it's all your bloody fault," I retorted angrily at her. "Next time, when I say we have to leave at a specific time to go somewhere, we *leave* at that specific time."

Bubbles held her head down and didn't say anything. However, after I had quickly calmed down, we got into conversation with a middle aged lady who had originally moved to St Cleer from Lancashire who lived on the other, posher side of the village and had asked if we, too, were local. When we told her that not only were we local but suffering from abuse because of it, she was quite stunned.

PART EIGHT
THE BEGINNING OF THE END

The ignorance and bigotry had now began to reach its' zenith and both Bubbles and I were suffering. We'd put on a brave face whenever we did go out.

"For St George and St England and don't let these redneck cunts get you down because they're thick, uneducated scum who would shit themselves if they went to a real estate," I used to tell her, trying to put a bit of encouragement in her. The stress was beginning to take its toll on us and we were often ill because of it. The rednecks would never ever have a go at me directly but would do it indirectly with Bubbles and that made it worse on my account.

One morning she had been walking towards the village bus stop when two white youths approached her.

"I still see you're going out with that black bastard then?"

He received an almighty punch to the face that sent him sprawling but he quickly got up and ran off along with his mate. Bubbles went after them. But in the space of a few seconds, they had disappeared completely and were nowhere to be seen.

When she reached home sometime later, I noticed that her knuckles on her right hand had been bruised.

"What the hell happened?" I enquired.

She explained what had happened earlier. "They won't say anything as I can't see the wankers admitting they got beaten up by a girl, can you? One of them I've seen a few times in the village so he must be local. The other one is an outsider. But they'll be keeping a low profile after this."

She was right. I was seething when she had told me this and I wanted to hunt them down but Bubbles never did see them again.

By now, I had given up on working for Re:Source and just stuck with working at the Bodmin and Wenford and another voluntary job I had started last year doing some gardening/kitchen assistant at the Stuart House heritage museum, a place where King Charles 1st once resided briefly there in 1644 during the (1st) English Civil War. The later job I thought was more satisfying and rewarding, even though I had to do (and successfully passed and received) a Food and Hygiene Level 2 certificate to officially work in the kitchen even though I have worked in many kitchens in previous jobs I've had. It's the new Health and Safety thing these days now and it's also a case of politically correctness gone completely fucking mad just to prove you can efficiently clean utensils in a kitchen. So I was out of the house and out of Bubbles' way most of the time, enjoying what little personal freedom I had.

One afternoon, however, when I got my usual bus home from the town centre back to St Cleer, the bus arrived at the usual Market Inn stop. Just before I got off, the bus driver, yet another bloody Brummie, only starts to imitate what I would call a pathetic attempt to do a West Indian accent (Jamaican Patrois).

"You have the wrong accent, mate," I said to him with apathy.

Us Leos have an unfortunate knack of letting our emotions run riot. I got home and then started bashing the hell out of a cushion on the sofa.

Bubbles heard the commotion and ran up. "Mick, Mick, what's wrong?"

"Oh, it's nothing, er-"

Bubbles stopped me right there. "You're going to tell me what's happened." She ended firmly. "Right now."

I told her about the Brummie bus driver and what had happened. She could scarcely believe what she was hearing.

"If that had happened in London or Manchester, he would've been beaten up on the spot. Incredible."

We phoned up Western Greyhound to make a complaint. Bubbles was told that "the complaint would be dealt with."

SPRING: LISKEARD MARKET FAIR

At certain periods during the year Liskeard has Market Fairs in the Fore Street area and you have traders selling all sorts of delicacies. We spent a fair bit and then decided to get the half three departure from Liskeard back to St Cleer.

Bubbles boarded the bus first with me behind her.

Unfortunately, it was the same Brummie Bastard that was the driver for this service and I knew immediately was going to happen.

He began his Jim Davidson Jamaican rant.

"Okay, well the first time you did that in front of me, it weren't funny. Now I'm telling you for the second and last time. Bloody cut it out, yeah."

"Oh, I'm only having a laugh, come on," protested Brummie Wanker.

"Yeah, well I don't find your particular humour very bloody funny," I shouted at him.

Instead of apologizing, I was told to sit down. Incensed, I sat down next to Bubbles, but also opposite an off-duty bus driver immediately to my right.

"See that cunt of a bus driver I told you about?" I said to Bubbles, who had heard the commotion and had enquired what the spat was all about. "That's the bastard the insulted me the first time two weeks ago."

Bubbles was grim and silent. She put a reassuring hand on my arm.

"This is what we're going to do", she said quietly.

        *   *   *   *   *   *   *

The following day we attended the local police station. The police woman was quite gobsmacked as this was the first case of its kind she had to deal with. Her remark was even more startling.

"I am really quite shocked by what you've told me and I am genuinely sorry you've suffered so much in our Duchy."
I tried to play it down. "Well, the way I see it, it's always been there, but no one talks about it. I guess I must be the first person strong enough to come out with it."

We left and went to make an appointment to see the local MP, Sheryl Murray, a conservative. Now, it has to be said that my bias against anything political went straight out of the window (at least, on a temporary basis) when we both saw her a week later at Liskeard's Conservative Club in nearby Pike Street. She, too, could hardly believe the facts being unravelled, and just like the police woman we saw a week ago, made a genuine apology.

Blimey, an MP that's apologetic, that's a new one!

She worked fast, and got results. Western Greyhound had been, as expected, useless and weren't interested in getting back to Bubbles. But within a week, due to Ms Murray's intervention, I received an official letter of apology from the bus company plus what looked like a scribbled letter of apology begrudgingly written by the bus driver himself.

We left it at that. We never saw that Brummie Bastard driver after that again. He obviously must've been transferred to an entirely different route altogether.

The next day, I wrote a small article about the two previous experiences about the two youths, the bus driver and St Cleer village life (well, the part of the village where we live anyway) to a local newsletter for publication. This had an immediate effect on anyone reading it, but it did have its consequences. I stood my ground and answered to anyone querying why I wrote the article, saying I was quite proud that I wrote it as certain issues had needed to be addressed. And I'd come out and did it. I hadn't stated any names, but everyone knew I'd wrote it anyway.

I got the backlash I was expecting in the form of Robbie Redneck from next door who accused me of calling him and the entire village racist and that people had been stopping him on the road calling him a racist.

Ok, so it's perfectly alright to call a Asian person a 'Paki', as you've mentioned before but not acceptable to be labelled a racist? You stupid dumbfuck, I thought. And this is the man that likes ska music and has a Michael Jackson doll in his house. When he had overstepped the mark by telling Bubbles that "if my back wasn't playing up, I would've dragged the both of you outside and giving you I hiding', I waited for him to arrive back at his house one afternoon while mowing the front lawn.

"Oi," I shouted at him. "You said to my missus that if your back wasn't playing up, you'd drag me and her outside to give me a smack, so I'm outside right now, right in front of you. Let's see you 'sort me out' as you said, right here, right now."

I don't think I've ever confronted anyone like this. But even mild mannered people like me have a breaking point.

"You put that article in the newsletter calling me a racist. I've had people from car windows stopping me and giving me grief."

Good, you wanker.

"Which point in the article does it *actually* say you are one? Read the article again, idiot."
"When you first came here I treated you decent, we went for pub meals, I let you into my home-"
"You WHAT? You stopped talking to us and began to ignore me straight after we attended that bloody party we went to last year. You have a big mouth and I know you've talked to people. One day that mouth of yours is going to get you into trouble. So keep that mouth of yours shut, you gossiping bastard."

I was really going the whole hog now. Not even Bubbles could stop me when I'm on form like this.

"So tell me who I've been talking to then?"
"The entire village and half of Liskeard, it would seem."

Bubbles was trying to usher me in but I was having none of it. The frustration and anger had finally boiled over at last and this bastard was getting the full force of it.

"You're a fucking prick, you know that?" continued Redneck.
"Don't you swear at me like that." How I had the urged to crack him one, especially after his next retort:
"It's my country, and I can say what I like." He had put himself right in it without realizing what he had just said. We glared at each other for a few seconds before he finally went in, slamming the door behind him.

SUMMER: CARNIVAL TIME

Don't be fooled into thinking that the annual St Cleer carnival is anything like the Notting Hill Carnival. It is NOTHING like the Notting Hill Carnival. Or any other carnival for that matter. It's a strictly local affair, its' origins dating back to the Second World War, but over the years, its' status has decreased more and more and is now a pale shadow of what it was in its' glory days. Me and Bubbles attended one the previous year and we weren't too impressed in all honestly. While we were sitting down on a granite fencing watching the procession go by on its way to the sports field just outside the village, I was being intensely stared at by someone who looked like one of those ghastly Hooray Henry royals parasites, following the floats in front of him with the crowd behind him. He reminded me of those daft Africans me and Bubbles encountered with their blank, zombiefied stares.

We were hoping he'd walk into the float directly in front of him and hurt himself, the bastard.

"Oi", I shouted out at him, with unremitted glee. "You keep on staring at me like that, your eyes will fall out!"
I'd never seen someone trying to compose and look dignified so quickly and he almost crashed into the float in front of him.

OCTOBER: THE END

"I've been in love. Painless, pointless and overrated."
Damon, 'The Vampire Diaries' Series 1, Episode 6

When it was time to pay the rent and Bubbles had yet again run into money problems and couldn't pay her share something inside me suddenly snapped.

"This is the last time I'm going to supplement you. From now on you're on your own."

She couldn't pay her share of the bills either. I had booked a week and a half holiday to stay in Hamburg, Germany to be with some friends as I could no longer bear to be in Bubbles' presence. I could've left her without any electricity in the house. Maybe she should've deserved it. But I paid up anyway. The phone had been cut off sometime back because I had refused to pay her share of the bill so I now relied on my mobile. I hadn't told her about my planned trip because it was no longer feasibly to have a decent conversation with her because everything she now said was questionable and half-truths, especially in the case of money.

When I came back from my break, I set about doing some flat hunting.

"I don't know whether to punch you or throw you through a plate-glass window," she remarked.

She tried just about every dirty trick in the window to stop me from leaving, but she had made her own downfall bed and slept on it. When I had made some final arrangements with an estate agent for a flat to rent in Devon, she had phoned them in my absence and tried in vain to stop them. When the estate agent then spoke to me in confidence about what had happened, I felt grim, but more determined to get away from her.

"What you did, speaking to the estate agent," I said to Bubbles apathetically. "It didn't work."

She then tried some half arsed story about some DHSS bloke coming round to the house to arrest me because my disability claim had been in question.

"Izzat so?" I scoffed. "You should know yourself that disability itself isn't just restricted to a physical thing, it's also a mental thing. So let him come. He won't get very far and neither will anyone else."

Of course, in the days that followed, no one had turned up, as expected.

A few days before my departure, she tried her last and lowest trick by phoning Mum when she had sneaked of into the kitchen while I was watching some tv and tried to persuade her to lend her £300 for the removal of her own belongings to go back to Lancashire.
Mum might be getting on in age, but she has a lot more suss than most people put together. She turned her down flat.

The final irony from her came on my penultimate day of living in St Cleer. I woke up early to get ready for work at the Bodmin and Wenford railway as usual. Bubbles had cleaned and pressed my shirt and jacket and there was nothing to indicate there was anything out of the ordinary that morning. I left, but when I got to the station, there were no heritage trains running so therefore there was no work for me and I realized I must've read the timetable wrong. I had the option of working with some signal staff, but I politely declined and travelled back home.

As I approached the cul-de-sac, I was surprised to see a large white van parked outside the house. I walked around it, to see Bubbles had already packed half her stuff with the help of the van driver.

I was left open mouthed but quickly restored my composure. "So you were just going to go, without even a word or a note? So I would've just come back to a half empty house if I hadn't come back home unexpectedly early?"

Bubbles was always excellent in the fact that she made up excuses on the spot. Maybe she had attended a 'School For Excuses of Any Situation' and past a bachelor's degree in it.

"I couldn't have called you because I had run out of credit on my mobile." (Later on she was to have said that after she had rushed to take out yet another loan the van bloke just turned up out of the blue after dismissing a pre-arrangement set time and day, which was pretty hard to swallow, even by her standards.)

After about another 20 minutes, and the packing had all been done, she climbed aboard the van and left, driving off into the distance and driving out of my life forever.
Suddenly, there was a great big void in my life. After spending two years living together, a great chunk had seemed to be torn from me. The house seemed like a morgue. I'd never known it so quiet. One minute Bubbles was there, the next minute, gone.
And she had taken my cats with her.

I sat down on the sofa, and feeling emotionless and blank, a tear suddenly escaped my left eye.

      *   *   *   *   *   *   *   *

The following afternoon, a van driver and his assistant that I had hired came to take my stuff to the new flat. I had wanted them to come in the morning or early afternoon but they couldn't make it until the evening, the time that I deliberately wanted to avoid. The final humiliation occurred when Robbie Redneck had called over one of his two faced friends I had been acquaintances with to watch me leave. I had some pride left and as she approached his house from her home across the cul-de-sac a few yards away, I ignored her and blanked both of them out. The bastards were having a right good laugh at my expense, but it would only be for about 20 minutes while I was loading my belongings.

And then...I was off.

I breathed a sigh of relief and the thought of never having to live in Cornwall ever again. Never having to meet and live with people like Robbie Redneck, the self-styled village patriarch, never having to meet arrogant Cockneys and arrogant Brummies. Never having to hear dogs constantly barking.

I don't have nightmares of Cornwall anymore. In fact, I can now laugh at the people that were part of my life and I can now laugh at how pathetic some people are. The moral of the story is: don't be too trusting and don't be too open with anyone.

It does sorta work if you put your mind to it....

"Being a good person can get you in a lot of trouble sometimes, especially when you don't know who to trust."
L.Ron Hubbard

The End

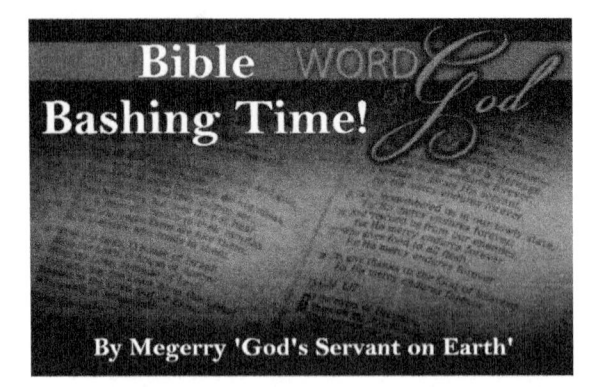

Bible Bashing Time!

By Megerry 'God's Servant on Earth'

Welcome to CORNWALL
Not far from England.
Not far enough.

Thick sounding ignorant Brummies and posh Cockneys?
Welcome to CORNWALL
You'll never escape.
KERNOW
a'gas dynergh

"Roz the Tyrant, she say:
"You will DO AS I SAY because I am in charge, I!"

This here's a broom.
B-R-O-O-M.
Brooooom.
Y'all gotta use two hands to use it properly, an' NOT one hand.

    Y'all got that?

        Good.

Harry Potter and the Prisoner of Liskeard

J. K. ROWLING

Harry finds that he'll need every ounce of magic to escape the hell of Liskeard...

HARRY POTTER and the case of the Cornish Dumbfucks

Liskeard. Mate, I wouldn't bother if I were you.

Richard **TROWBRIDGE**
estate & letting agents
We'll stitch you up big time.

Welcome to
Liskeard
You'd wish you'd never got off. Seriously.
This station is unfortunately operated by: First Great Western

Way Out
Lounge & Toilets
Looe Trains (Platform 3)

The astoundingly fantastic and multi award winning St Cleer Parish Carnival.
I woudn't worry too much about it though, it's cack.

These buses break down often, you know.

Storm.
The loudest dog in the village.

St Cleer Well. Typical modern housing spoils the background.

Carbis Bay

Printed in Great Britain
by Amazon